3-MINUTE DAILY DEVOTIONS

A 365 Devotional
for Teen Girls

Written by
Jennifer McCaman

B&H
PUBLISHING GROUP
Nashville, Tennessee

God's Word

A girl's best friend is not a diamond, it's the Word of God. When it comes to knowing how to live, nothing is more powerful than Scripture. The Bible helps us recognize lies, gives us energy, and shows us how to live. In this section, we will get to know the value of the Bible and its power in our lives.

DAY 1

Lie Detector

Keep me from the way of deceit and graciously give me your instruction. (Psalm 119:29)

Almost every girl owns a fake diamond. They're sparkly, cheap, and most people can't tell the difference. If you tried to sell that fake diamond to a jewelry store, they would spot it in a second. Know why? It's because they're experts in real diamonds. They know the exact weight, color, and cut of an authentic gem.

As followers of Christ, when we spend time studying the Word of God, we know what truth is. We know what God says will bring us happiness and what will bring us misery. Then when someone—our friends, magazines, movies, songs—tries to tell us something that goes against God's Word, we recognize it as a cheap lie. Study the Bible. Know what God teaches, and you will can recognize the fakes when they try to deceive you.

DAY 2

Source for Purity

*God—his way is perfect; the word of the L*ᴏʀᴅ *is pure.*
He is a shield to all who take refuge in Him. (Psalm 18:30)

Have you ever been drinking a cool glass of water and all of a sudden you see a bug in your glass? It's terrible! You don't just get the bug out and keep on drinking (that's something boys would do); you throw the whole glass of water away and gag several times. We want to drink pure water, no bugs included. The Word of God is like pure water to our souls. When we read it and live it out, it nourishes our hearts and tells us where to find joy. The world offers us dirty water to drink. Movies, TV, and social media tell us how to live and what's popular, but their water is disgusting. It offers no truth and no lasting happiness. When you drink it, you get spiritually and emotionally sick. Drink the Word of God by reading it and obeying it—it is pure, and it will make you pure too.

DAY 3

Cure for a Dusty Day

My life is down in the dust;
give me life through your word. (Psalm 119:25)

Have you ever breathed in a mouthful of dust? First of all, it's disgusting. You're breathing in who knows what kind of filth. It's also choking—it fills your nose and lungs so you can't breathe. You have to sneeze or cough to get it out. Some days are dusty. The stuff of the world—worry, fear, insecurity, frustrations—fills our hearts and minds until we can't see clearly. It chokes out the things of God and covers us with filth. The cure for a dusty day? The Word of God. When we go to His Word, we're reminded of the love of God and His plan for us. We read stories of how much God loves us and His promises. The Word of God blasts the dust off our hearts and minds. The words of God are a fresh, clean breath of air for our souls. The next time you feel overwhelmed with the dust of the world, run to God's Word. He is the cure for every dusty day.

DAY 4

He Helps Us Understand

*Open my eyes so that I may contemplate wondrous things
from your instruction. (Psalm 119:18)*

*Teach me, Lᴏʀᴅ, the meaning of your statutes,
and I will always keep them. (Psalm 119:33)*

Have you ever tried to read a book for school that you totally didn't understand? Why does the author have to use such complicated language? Can't they just speak plain English? A lot of girls feel the same way about the Bible. Many girls want to read the Bible, but they think it's just too hard to understand. Don't worry, God totally understands. He wants to help you. The Bible says that the Lord will teach us the meaning of His Word. He is the one who opens our eyes to the Scriptures. He's also placed people in your life to help you understand, like your parents, your Sunday school teachers, and your pastor. The more you ask questions and try to understand, the more your eyes will be opened to what the Bible is actually saying. So don't get discouraged. Just keep reading. Before long, you will be teaching someone else how to understand God's words.

DAY 5

Theme Song

*Your statutes are the theme of my song
during my earthly life. (Psalm 119:54)*

Every good show has a theme song. It's catchy, it gets stuck in your head, and it tells us all about what the show will be about. Did you know that your life has a theme song? It tells the world who you are and what you're about. Some girls have a sad, gloomy theme song. Some girls have an adventurous one. The Bible says that God's Word is to be our theme song. That means we're known for our love for God and our obedience to Him. When we let God write our theme song, the world knows who we are and where we stand. Let the words of God and the character of God be the song over your life. It's the most beautiful song you will ever live by.

DAY 6

Cure for Grief

I am weary from grief;
strengthen me through your word. (Psalm 119:28)

Grief is more powerful than sadness or having a bad day. It saturates everything you do all day. Grief is exhausting because it occupies every corner of your thoughts and every one of your feelings. The only source stronger than grief is the Word of God. It will breathe life into even the darkest place in your life. When you are sad beyond explanation, God's Word will encourage you. He knows your pain, and He alone has the ability to make you strong again. Run to His arms and look to His Word. He will strengthen you again and walk with you in the pain.

DAY 7

Key to Happiness and Joy

How happy are those whose way is blameless,
who walk according to the Lord's instruction! (Psalm 119:1)

Have you ever been friends with a rain cloud? A rain cloud friend mopes around all day, constantly complaining about her life and her problems. She's always crying, never smiling, and no one even knows what her laugh sounds like. As followers of Christ, we don't have to be rain clouds. We have the key to real joy and true purpose. As Christians, we get to laugh harder and have more than the world. When we follow the Lord, we don't have to walk around with frowns. We have the key to true happiness. We know real joy and lasting love. We know our Creator, and we were saved by Jesus. We all have rain-cloud days, but when we return to the presence of God, that sadness melts away in the light of the joy of the Lord.

DAY 8

Storm Shelter

He is a shield to those who take refuge in him. (Proverbs 30:5)

Storm shelters are designed to withstand powerful natural disasters. They can hold up under hurricane winds and stay standing in a tornado. We usually stock them with water, batteries, canned goods, and even pet food (nobody wants Scrappy to blow away). God designed a storm shelter for our souls. When the winds of stress, temptation, and evil blow against us, we don't have to crumble. He is our shield and our place of safety where we can run when we feel overwhelmed or worried. He longs to cover us when the storm rages all around us. What is your storm shelter right now? Make it the Lord and you will have peace in the fiercest storm.

DAY 9

GPS for Life

*All Scripture is inspired by God and is profitable
for teaching, for rebuking, for correcting,
for training in righteousness. (2 Timothy 3:16)*

Have you ever gotten lost with a parent who is really bad with directions? Maybe the GPS stopped working and the phones are dead. Everyone gets really stressed out. Your mom or dad tries to remember which way to turn, or tries to turn around, but suddenly all the roads look alike. The exact same thing can happen in our lives. When we don't have a clear sense of spiritual direction, wrong choices can seem right. Voices try to point us in the right direction, but they only get us further lost. The absolute best spiritual GPS for your life is the Word of God. In the Bible, God gives us directions that guide us to be godly. He tells us exactly what will bring us joy and what will bring us pain. He gives us stories of people who obeyed God and stories of people who didn't. It is the only perfect guide for your life. Want to have a strong sense of spiritual direction? Study the Bible. It will direct you all the days of your life.

DAY 10

Plugged In

He answered, "It is written: Man must not live on bread alone but on every word that comes from the mouth of God." (Matthew 4:4)

Have you ever had a piece of technology die at the worst time? Maybe your phone died right when you needed to call your mom. Maybe your computer crashed exactly when you needed to print out a paper for school. No matter how new and expensive a piece of technology is, it's worthless if it isn't charged. We are the same way. We draw our energy and strength from the Word of God. His Word fuels us to know Him more and to know His commands so we can have joy. If we're not plugged into His Word and His presence, we're like an iPad with a dead battery—we just sit there, useless. Are you connected to the true source of spiritual energy and joy? If not, plug into God. He is ready to give you all the strength and power you need for the day.

DAY 11

More Valuable Than Gold and Diamonds

Instruction from your lips is better for me than thousands of gold and silver pieces. (Psalm 119:72)

What if someone hid several one-hundred dollar bills in your room and you had one minute to find them all? Girl, you would tear that room to pieces. You would pull your bed apart, empty your drawers, and destroy your closet until you found that stash of cash. What would happen if we put that same kind of energy into seeking God? What if we poured ourselves into knowing Him more and learning more about Him? We can do it. His presence and His word are more valuable than any stack of one-hundred dollar bills. His love never fails. His presence is the answer to all our problems. His protection and guidance protect us in the face of our evil world. Every day we have a choice in how much we will seek God. Let's seek Him with our whole heart, and we will find true riches.

DAY 12

Protection from Sin

I have treasured your word in my heart so that
I may not sin against you. (Psalm 119:11)

Have you ever been tricked into playing a game you didn't understand? When you don't know the rules, how can you be any good? You're going to lose every time. That's exactly what the enemy wants for you. He wants you to wander through your day living by your own feelings and guesses. The less you know about God's Word, the less you'll know how to make wise decisions. God longs for you to know His Word and treasure it in your heart. When you know His guide for living, you can avoid sin and glorify your Father in everything you do. His Word helps us learn how to make wise choices and how to avoid wrong ones. It helps us know how to treat people and how to trust God. Hide His Word in your heart, and you will have everything you need to live for Him.

DAY 13

Shot of Energy

Let the word of Christ dwell richly among you, in all wisdom teaching and admonishing one another through psalms, hymns, and spiritual songs, singing to God with gratitude in your hearts. (Colossians 3:16)

Have you ever tried an energy drink? They have tons more caffeine than coffee or regular soda, and they're actually pretty bad for you. They can make even the sleepiest girl suddenly wide-awake and even crazy hyper. God's Word acts like an energy drink for our spirits. When you're feeling sad, an encouraging Bible verse can lift your spirit faster than a hundred Monster cans. Scripture can also add a spark to your gloomy friends the next time they're having a bad day. The Word of God is living and active and able to change your mood. The next time you or your friends are down, encourage each other with a Bible verse, and let the Word of God jolt you out of a bad day.

Passion for Purity

Purity starts by letting Christ capture your heart. He alone is our source for mental, emotional, spiritual, and physical purity. This section is about discovering the key to purity and guarding it with all your heart.

DAY 14

Key to Purity

How can a young man keep his way pure?
By keeping your word. (Psalm 119:9)

In a world that shoves immodesty and all kinds of sin in our faces, how can a young lady keep her way pure? It doesn't happen by accident. The map to purity is found in the Word of God. Do you want to honor God with your eyes, heart, mind, and body? Search the Word of God. It shows us what to stay away from and what to let in our lives. It also shows us how to desire purity so it brings us joy. God's Word speaks of the importance of godly friends and honoring your parents. You are absolutely beautiful before the Lord. He is your protector and the only one able to guide you to the path of purity. Trust Him with your purity and walk in His ways.

DAY 15

Strength in Running Away

For this is God's will, your sanctification:
that you keep away from sexual immorality. (1 Thessalonians 4:3)

Flee sexual immorality! Every other sin a person commits is outside
the body, but the person who is sexually immoral sins against his
own body. (1 Corinthians 6:18)

Sometimes God tells us to stand and fight, and other times He tells us to run away. When it comes to sexual immorality, God tells us to run for our lives. God designed sex to be between a man and woman in marriage. Everything else is sin. Sexual sin tries to invade every area of our lives: music, movies, magazines, and Web sites. We have to be on guard about what we let into our minds. Sexual purity starts in your heart and mind. What movies do you watch? What music do you listen to? What posters are on your bedroom walls? It matters because what you put in your mind will come out in your life. Run away from sexual immorality. Trust your parents to guard your heart when they say a certain movie, concert, or TV show is off limits, even when you don't understand. This is one area of sin we don't need to study or try to fight against—we just need to run away.

DAY 16

A Pure Mind

*We demolish arguments and every proud thing that
is raised up against the knowledge of God, and we take
every thought captive to obey Christ. (2 Corinthians 10:4–5)*

If you've ever had a splitting headache, you know it impacts everything you do. You can't do school work or play sports. You can't eat or hang out with your friends. Headaches affect your whole body. In the same way, your mind impacts your spiritual life. If you put unholy things into your mind, your entire spiritual life suffers. Your mind affects your purity. Be on guard against the movies, TV, and the Internet sites you put into your mind. Living a pure life starts with keeping your mind pure before the Lord. The world is full of opportunities to fill your mind with unholy things—things that give you a serious spiritual headache. Fight to set pure things before your eyes and to keep your mind focused on the Lord. Your whole spiritual life is influenced by your mind, so fill it with the things of the Lord.

DAY 17

Pure Words

Every word of God is pure. (Proverbs 30:5)

In the movie *Up*, the villains are these scary bad dogs that talk through their collars. Then the scary leader dog's collar breaks and he suddenly talks in a squeaky high mouse voice. It's funny because the words he says don't match who he's supposed to be at all.

If we want to be pure, our words have to match who we are in Christ. The words we speak have everything to do with our purity. If we look godly and act godly, but speak evil words, it ruins our character all the way through. Part of having pure words means avoiding bad language, inappropriate joking, and tearing down other people. Being pure doesn't just happen in one part of our lives; it's who we are in every area, and that includes the words we speak. Take every word you speak before the Lord and make sure it pleases Him and reflects who He is in your life.

DAY 18

Pure Body

For this is God's will, your sanctification: that you keep away from sexual immorality, that each of you knows how to control his own body in holiness and honor. (1 Thessalonians 4:3–4)

The world teaches that love and sexual activity go together, but God's Word says something different. God created sex to be between a man and a woman inside the commitment of marriage. Sexual activity in any other context is wrong and will lead to incredible hurt and pain. Maybe you've never had a boyfriend and can't imagine ever feeling tempted to dishonor God in this way. That's why it's so awesome that you learn God's truth now, before you ever begin to date. When you hide God's Word about purity in your heart, you will know it by the time you begin to date. Trust His truth about marriage and sex, and honor God in purity. Learn these truths when you're young and cling to them. They will protect you and keep you from experiencing a whole lot of pain.

DAY 19

The Root of Purity

He said to him, "Love the Lord your God with all your heart, with all your soul, and with all your mind. This is the greatest and most important command." (Matthew 22:37–38)

The root of purity is loving God with all your heart. When God has captured your heart, you will have no appetite for impure things. We don't dress modestly and guard our minds because it's just something Christians do. We do these things because we love God so much and trust that He wants to protect us from pain. When you've found real love in Christ, you won't be tempted by cheap, fake loves that give shallow promises. Right now, focus your energy and attention on falling in love with God. He will guard your heart better than anyone else. Obey His Word and your parents, even when you don't fully understand. Purity isn't about keeping a list of rules so you'll be a "good girl." It's falling so passionately in love with God that nothing the world offers can distract from that love. Love God. Obey Him. Purity will follow.

DAY 20

A Perfect Match

Don't become partners with those who do not believe. For what partnership is there between righteousness and lawlessness? Or what fellowship does light have with darkness? (2 Corinthians 6:14)

Have you ever been playing a board game and your mom makes your baby brother or sister be on your team? It's really annoying because they don't know how to play. You do all the work and try to keep them from messing things up or eating the pieces. You're definitely not real partners. God's Word says that's why Christians should only date and marry other Christians. Only a Christian can understand and build up another Christian. When a Christian dates a non-believer, they have nothing in common. Their very reasons for living are different. A non-Christian does not understand God's views on salvation, money, joy, or real love. Even if you haven't started dating yet, decide now that you will only date other Christians, guys who are passionate about seeking God. Any guy who tries to pursue you must also be pursuing Jesus. Making this decision right now will protect your heart in a huge way.

Temptation

Temptation is the draw to do something you know is wrong. Sometimes the desire to sin is strong, but God is always stronger. This section deals with some of the temptations all girls face and how to overcome them in Christ.

DAY 21

Pretty Little Lies

The righteous hate lying, but the wicked bring disgust and shame.
(Proverbs 13:5)

White lies. It's a term we use to mean a tiny lie that doesn't hurt anyone. According to God, there's no such thing as white lies. The truth matters whether it's shouted on stage in front of thousands or silent during a test at school. Lies are always wrong, and they always cause pain. Lies might offer an easy escape, but they do great spiritual damage. Let's love God so much that lies have no place in our lives. The next time you have the chance to tell a white lie, make the harder choice and tell the whole truth. It may bring some temporary pain, but it will definitely bring you more joy in the long run.

DAY 22

I'm Not Buying It

Therefore, put to death what belongs to your earthly nature: sexual immorality, impurity, lust, evil desire, and greed, which is idolatry.
(Colossians 3:5)

Greed is like a slimy snake that slithers quietly into our lives. We don't realize it until it's wrapped itself around us. Greed is wanting more stuff. It's looking at your own stuff and thinking, *I hate my clothes, my computer is as old as a dinosaur, and I wish I had a bigger room*. Greed is a sickness of the heart, a continual state of dissatisfaction. You want whatever you see and you dislike whatever you get—an endless circle that coils around your life. Greed chokes out the work of God because it's the opposite of a godly life. As followers of Christ, we have to be on guard against greed. We have to constantly tell ourselves that we're happy with what we have, that we don't need to get caught up in wanting more. When you practice being thankful and cherish the things you do have, you will destroy greed and keep it from choking out the work of God in your life.

DAY 23

No More Potty Mouth

But now, put away all the following:
anger, wrath, malice, slander, and filthy language
from your mouth. (Colossians 3:8)

Imagine a large ice-cold drink of your favorite soda. What if someone took just a tiny teaspoon of mud and sprinkled it into your drink. Unless you're crazy, you're not taking one sip of that soda. A tiny sprinkle of something gross poisons the whole drink. It's the same way with our language. Every word you say matters. Girls, if we claim to follow Christ, we must take every word captive before Him. Let us not have anything to do with curse words or filthy language. Even one ugly word can poison your image and your influence for Christ. It's true the world has no problem with cussing, but the world does not know Christ. Choose to be different, because every word matters.

DAY 24

I Really (Don't) Need a Boyfriend

"For God loved the world in this way:
He gave his one and only Son, so that everyone who believes
in him will not perish but have eternal life." (John 3:16)

The world tells you from a young age that you're incomplete without a boyfriend. They say that even young girls need to pour all their energy into calling, texting, chasing, and flirting with boys. Don't buy into this lie. The truth is that Christ alone completes us. He is everything we need for security and love—not a guy. Practice trusting God now with your whole heart. Trust Him to be your love story. Don't throw yourself at boys to get attention. Whatever joy you get from that will not last. The Lord offers complete and lasting joy. Long before you start to date, let the Lord capture your heart. Trust your parents' boundaries about dating, and trust your heart to the Lord. He will protect it always.

DAY
25

We Bow Down

So then, my dear friends, flee from idolatry. (1 Corinthians 10:14)

In other religions, people bow down and offer sacrifices of food and drink to statues representing their gods. This is called idolatry, meaning the worship of false gods, or idols. In our culture, we don't bow down to gold statues, but we definitely worship false gods. Some of the idols a girl might worship are clothes, beauty, money, a guy, popularity, strength, and the praise of others. Our biggest idol usually stares back at us from the mirror—ourselves. We worship these gods by serving them with our attention and energy. We desire them more than everything else. The Bible says to flee from false idols. Only Jesus deserves your worship. We were created to worship the one true God, and we will be miserable until He has our whole heart. Pay attention to the false gods demanding your worship. Just because you don't bow down to your new shoes or your friends doesn't mean you don't worship them. Guard your heart and never let any idol come between you and God.

DAY 26

Dragging It into the Light

Don't participate in the fruitless works of darkness,
but instead expose them. (Ephesians 5:11)

Have you ever walked downstairs to a creepy basement at night? What happens when you suddenly turn on the light? Every disgusting, creepy bug runs away. Basement bugs usually hate the light and want to get away from it. Sin is the same way. Sin thrives in places where it's dark and secret. When you shine the light of God's presence, into it, it runs away. If you're struggling with sin—lying, greed, gossiping—take your sin before God. Pray about it and confess it to the Lord. Pray about it with your parents and Christian friends. It's tempting to try to deal with sin yourself, in secret, but this never works because sin loves the dark. When you drag sin into the light of God, it will not survive.

DAY 27

Stronger Than You Realize

Therefore, submit to God. Resist the devil,
and he will flee from you. (James 4:7)

In Christ, you are stronger than you realize. The Bible says when you stand up to Satan and do not fall to temptation, he will run away from you. When you want to say something mean to your little brother but you don't, when you're tempted to lie to your parents but you tell the truth, when you stand up to a bully at school instead of joining in the teasing, you are resisting the devil. Every time you show him some spiritual muscle, he runs away and hides. He is terrified of the power of Christ in you. So instead of giving in to temptation, stand strong for God and the enemy will run away from you like a scared puppy.

DAY
28

The Enemy's Goal for You

But I fear that, as the serpent deceived Eve by his cunning, your minds may be seduced from a sincere and pure devotion to Christ.
(2 Corinthians 11:3)

The enemy's biggest goal every day isn't to get you to commit some big sin like lying or stealing. His number one goal is to keep you from being close to God. That's it. If he can keep you from loving God and drawing close to Him, he will get you to sin. The best way to fight sin in your life and to experience the blessings of God is to just stay close to God. Keep your pure devotion to Christ by praying, sharing your heart with God, reading the Bible, and worshiping Him. When you have a close walk with God, nothing can come between that. Even when you sin, you quickly want to ask forgiveness. Keep your walk with God strong and you can handle any attack the enemy throws your way.

DAY 29

Dare to Kill Your Pride

To fear the LORD is to hate evil. I hate arrogant pride,
evil conduct, and perverse speech. (Proverbs 8:13)

There's a false romance trying to overtake every girl. It begs to be worshipped and adored, and it demands our undivided attention. You can find this false love simply by looking in a mirror. Every girl faces the temptation to be selfish, to seek her own needs above the needs of her family, and to make everything in life about her. Pride is not the same thing as confidence. Confidence is knowing you are a daughter of God and feeling good about yourself. Pride is thinking you're better than other people. Pride is a poison that will choke out the Spirit of God in your life. It blinds you to the needs of other people. Pride is also usually short-lived. As soon as someone makes fun of you, pride shatters and you're left feeling miserable. Scripture says God hates pride because of what it does to us. Kill the sin of pride in your life. Never think you're better than others, and remember that everything you have—your beauty, your personality, your friends, your stuff—is a gift from God, given to you so you can serve others.

DAY 30

Breaking Insecurity

He leads the humble in what is right and teaches them his way.
(Psalm 25:9)

Humility is a beautiful characteristic of every godly girl. Humility is thinking of others before yourself and putting your needs last. Insecurity, however, is not humility and does not please God. When you're insecure, you put yourself down. You don't like your hair, your body, or your personality. You talk and think badly about yourself. Insecurity is something every girl faces, but it's possible to overcome in Christ. The closer you get to God, the more confidence you have in Him. You realize that He made you exactly as you are and He is delighted with you. In His love, those insecurities melt away. When you're close to God, you actually like yourself more—not in a prideful way, but in a good way. You know who you are and you want to serve God. Although it seems strange, humility and confidence actually go together. The more confident you are in yourself, the less you need to be the center of attention and the more you can focus on other people's needs. Seek Christ and His confidence, and let Him blast away the insecurities in your life.

When I Sin

As we follow Christ, we will make mistakes. It's important that we know what to do when we fall so we can get back up. This section focuses on how to run back to God when you sin, and how to experience His forgiveness.

DAY
31

Inside a Stinky Fish

The Lord appointed a great fish to swallow Jonah, and Jonah was in the belly of the fish three days and three nights. (Jonah 1:17)

Sometimes when we disobey God it gets us in really big trouble. Nobody understands this better than Jonah. God told Jonah to do something, he tried to hide from God, and a big fish swallowed him whole. Jonah ended up doing exactly what God asked him to do in the first place. We can save ourselves a lot of pain if we just obey God the first time. He loves us so much and wants us to have great joy in obeying Him. When we run from God, we invite pain into our lives. A big fish might not swallow us, but we can definitely get a broken heart and damage the people around us. Obey God the first time and you will save yourself a lot of hurt.

DAY 32

What Makes God Vomit

I know your works, that you are neither cold nor hot. I wish that you were cold or hot. So, because you are lukewarm, and neither hot nor cold, I am going to vomit you out of my mouth. (Revelation 3:15–16)

There's a kind of sin God hates worse than open rebellion. The Bible says it actually makes Him want to vomit. The thing God hates worse than deliberate disobedience is being lukewarm. Being lukewarm means you follow God, but not all the way. You say you're a Christian, and you go to church, but you still look and act like the world. Refuse to be lukewarm. If you're going to follow God, do it with your whole heart. Love Him with all your mind, all your strength, and all your soul. So many girls say they love God, but their lives and their actions don't show it. Don't be like this. Trust God enough that you jump in all the way with Him. Run after Him and seek Him with everything you are, and He will bless you more than you could ever imagine.

DAY 33

The Accuser Is Silent

Then I heard a loud voice in heaven say, The salvation and the power and the kingdom of our God and the authority of his Christ have now come, because the accuser of our brothers and sisters, who accuses them before our God day and night, has been thrown down. (Revelation 12:10)

Nobody likes a tattletale. When your little sister or brother tattles on you, you just want to make them pay. We also have a tattler when it comes to our spiritual lives. The Bible says that Satan is the great accuser, meaning he stands before God and points out all our sin and flaws before God. He doesn't have to lie because we really are evil. We really mess up, and we really have tons of sins every single day. But when we come to Christ, He covers our sins. His blood removes our guilt and sin from our hearts. The Bible says that the Accuser is thrown down, meaning he has no more things to tattle about. He can no longer accuse us of sin because Christ took our sins away. That's something to celebrate and something to remember every day.

Not a Slave to Sin

*They promise them freedom, but they themselves
are slaves of corruption, since people are enslaved
to whatever defeats them. (2 Peter 2:19)*

Slavery isn't just something that we learn about in a history book. There are real slaves all over the world today, people who have been captured or tricked into giving away their freedom. Along with the tragedy of physical slaves, there are spiritual slaves. Everyone who does not know Christ is a slave. They might not wear chains on their hands, but they absolutely have a chain on their hearts. The Bible says that people are slaves of corruption and slaves to anything that defeats them. Whatever you worship—money, popularity, yourself—is what enslaves you. Only the power of Christ can set you free from spiritual slavery. Who is your master? Let it be Christ. When you lead others to Christ, you are helping them break the chains of a lifetime of slavery.

DAY 35

Lifted from the Slimy Pit

He brought me up from a desolate pit, out of the muddy clay, and set my feet on a rock, making my steps secure. (Psalm 40:2)

Imagine wearing your favorite outfit to school. You look super cute and you're ready to face the day, when all of a sudden you trip and fall in a giant muddy puddle. Your jeans are ruined, your shirt is splattered, and your shoes are gross. It's a terrible feeling. The only thing you can think about is *Get me out! And get this stuff off me!* The Bible says that God lifted us out of the muddy pit. Before we came to Christ, we lived in a pit of disgusting sin. The mud and the filth covered us, invaded out thoughts, our words, and our attitudes. The blood of Christ is the only thing able to clean our sins permanently and completely. In Him, we are clean. Don't return to the mud of your old sins. Walk securely in the love and life God has for you when you follow Him.

DAY 36

Get Real

For troubles without number have surrounded me; my iniquities have overtaken me; I am unable to see. They are more than the hairs of my head, and my courage leaves me. (Psalm 40:12)

I love God's Word because it's honest. Whatever you're feeling, you can trust that God's Word will apply to your life. These verses probably aren't ones you want to stencil on your bedroom wall, but they show the honesty of the Bible. Here, we see the psalmist struggling with sin. He feels afraid and surrounded by troubles. Instead of trying to deal with them on his own, however, he takes his fears to God. He pours out his heart before God, even though it's ugly. Sweet girl, whenever you feel broken or afraid, you can always run to God. You don't have to be in a good mood or fake a smile. He knows what's in your heart and He hears your prayers. So the next time you feel bad, be like the psalmist and tell it to God. He hears every word, and He will come to your rescue.

DAY 37

"If Only" Moments

"If only you had paid attention to my commands. Then your peace would have been like a river, and your righteousness like the waves of the sea." (Isaiah 48:18)

Do you ever wish you could go back in time and change one tiny wrong decision you made? If only you hadn't been friends with that person, if only you had kept your eyes on your own test, if only you hadn't said that to your sister. We all have those "if only" moments. We can't change the past, but we can absolutely change the future. Let your past mistakes fuel you to make good choices today. Just because you messed up yesterday doesn't mean you have to mess up today. God is able to give you a fresh start and a new day. Keep your eyes on Christ and obey His Word, and you will have way fewer "if only" moments.

Hating What God Hates

To fear the LORD is to hate evil. I hate arrogant pride,
evil conduct, and perverse speech. (Proverbs 8:13)

When someone makes fun of your best friend, how do you react? You get involved! Nobody treats your friend that way. Your best friend's enemy is your enemy too. That's how real friendship works. When you follow Christ, you begin to hate the same things He hates, and you love the things He loves. The closer you get to God, the more you hate lying, arrogance, bullying, gossip, and selfishness. You can't stand those things. You can tell how close someone is to God by how her desires line up with God's desires. You want to do the will of God, and you want to destroy any temptations that try to attack you. Do you want to hate evil and desire good? Draw close to God. Your desires will transform in His presence.

DAY 39

Not Abusing Grace

What should we say then? Should we continue in sin
so that grace may multiply? Absolutely not!
How can we who died to sin still live in it? (Romans 6:1–2)

Have you ever tried to get away with something at your grandparent's house that you would totally get busted for at your own house? Grandparents tend to be more easy-going about TV, candy, and bedtimes. They're quick to forgive and quick to give in. God is also quick to forgive, but that doesn't mean we get to take advantage of that grace. In fact, the more we know God, the more we want to avoid sin at all costs. He changes our appetites to desire the things He loves and hate the things He hates. Also, just because God forgives us doesn't mean we don't have consequences for sin. When you cheat on a test, God will forgive you, but you're still probably going to get a zero. Don't try to get away with sin. Seek to love God more, and ask Him to change your desires to match His.

DAY 40

Dead to Sin

*So, you too consider yourselves dead to sin but
alive to God in Christ Jesus. (Romans 6:11)*

Have you ever had a really bad virus—one that just made you feel miserable? What if you went to the doctor and he agreed to give you medicine to kill most of the virus but not all of it. You would think that doctor was insane. When you get sick, you want the whole virus killed! You want to feel better, so you want every germ destroyed. That's exactly how we're supposed to treat sin in our lives. God doesn't want to kill most of your sin; He wants to kill it all. He also doesn't want to hide it away just in case you need it later. He wants to destroy every single thing in your life that goes against His holiness. What sin do you still keep alive in your life? Telling lies? Pride? A bad attitude toward your parents? Hateful words toward your siblings? Don't let sin stay alive any more or it will make you sick. Trust God to kill all of it so you can be totally alive in Christ.

DAY 41

When I Keep Messing Up

For I do not understand what I am doing, because I do not practice what I want to do, but I do what I hate. (Romans 7:15)

Have you ever really wanted to follow God, but you kept messing up? Paul, the author of much of the New Testament, totally understood. He was a godly man, but he still struggled with sin. Just because you mess up doesn't mean you're cut off from God. God celebrates your steps of obedience. He doesn't yell at you for falling down. More than anything He wants your heart. Don't let your sin keep you from running to God for forgiveness. He loves you, and He is near to you when you fall. We don't have to do it on our own. The next time you mess up in your walk with God, don't stay down—run to God. Confess your sins and continue growing in your love for Him.

DAY 42

True Tears

For godly grief produces a repentance that leads to salvation without regret, but worldly grief produces death. (2 Corinthians 7:10)

When a girl gets in trouble, she can cry two kinds of tears. Either she cries godly tears because she feels bad, or she cries selfish tears because she got caught. The Bible says that when you cry because you're heartbroken over your sin, God is working in your life. This is "godly grief." It's godly because it means you realize how serious your mistake was and you never want to offend God like that again. Selfish tears mean you're sad in the moment, but you're not truly broken over your sin. Conviction—feeling bad about your sins—comes from the Holy Spirit. The next time you get in trouble, ask God to give you brokenness over your sin. He will give you godly tears and help you to stay away from that sin the next time it comes around.

DAY 43

Holy Amnesia

*"I sweep away your transgressions for my own
sake and remember your sins no more." (Isaiah 43:25)*

When you come to Christ, God not only forgives your sins, He forgets them. It's as if they never existed. The blood of Christ alone pays the price for your sins. The sacrifice of Christ, applied to your life, washes you clean. You are no longer enslaved to sins like meanness, rage, gossip, or lying. You are free to follow Christ and be close to Him. You're also free from the guilt of past sins. If God doesn't remember your sins, why should you? If you follow Christ, you are a new creation, free from sin, and able to live the Christian life to the glory of God? Are you still clinging to sin or the guilt of sin? Let God sweep away the sin and the guilt so you can live for Him in perfect forgiveness.

DAY 44

The Sound of Broken Chains

*He brought them out of darkness and gloom
and broke their chains apart. (Psalm 107:14)*

A modern girl's chains aren't made of metal. The chains that hold us down are invisible, but just as strong. Our chains are made from the hatred of our bodies, the desire to be popular, or the longing for more stuff. We're enslaved by the chains of selfishness, greed, insecurity, and pride. Sometimes we're just chained to the mirror, dragging around our own insecurities and desperate desire to be beautiful to someone. Christ alone can break these chains and set you free. You don't have to be a captive anymore. He longs to replace your chains with His power, His freedom, and His love. Chains always come with the darkest gloom. Come to the presence of God and every chain that holds you will come crashing down.

DAY 45

You Can't Judge Me!

"Do not judge, so that you won't be judged. For you will be judged by the same standard by which you judge others, and you will be measured by the same measure you use." (Matthew 7:1–2)

Have you ever felt like you were constantly standing on stage while other people judged your performance? You get judged by coaches, teachers, parents, and friends. Sometimes the stress of feeling like you have to be perfect is overwhelming. It can feel like God is judging you too. He's not. In Christ, you are judged by His obedience, not your disobedience, so you no longer have to fear spiritual judgment. Your sins were paid for on the cross, and the punishment of sin fell on Jesus. You are free from having to measure up. That doesn't mean you don't feel conviction for sin. When you disobey God, you still have consequences, but that discipline is from love, not the wrath of God. Your parents have a responsibility to help you be more like Christ, and that means disciplining you when you need it. That's not judgment; it's teaching. So the next time you feel like the whole world is judging you, know that God is not. Through Christ, you are good enough already. You are free to know Him and obey Him without fear of being judged.

The Smarts

Sometimes a girl can make straight As and still not be very smart. True wisdom is only found in Christ. This section focuses on how to get real wisdom through seeking God.

DAY 46

Young and Wise

The fear of the LORD is the beginning of knowledge; fools despise wisdom and discipline. (Proverbs 1:7)

The world describes a toolbox of intelligence filled with thick books, advanced math classes, a straight-A report card, and great test scores. These are the things the world thinks you need to be wise. In the Bible, God gives us another toolbox for wisdom that doesn't look anything like the world's. According to Scripture, the beginning of all wisdom isn't good grades, education, or reading big books—it's fearing the Lord. When you love God with your whole heart and seek Him, you will be wise. Your life will start to look like the life of Christ as you act, speak, and think like Him. Most girls want to be wise; they just look for wisdom in the wrong place. Nothing is wrong with making good grades or studying hard, but true wisdom only comes from seeking God. Seek Him with everything you are and you will find true wisdom that will guard you throughout your whole life.

DAY 47

Book-Smart versus God-Smart

The wisdom from above is first pure, then peace-loving, gentle, compliant, full of mercy and good fruits, unwavering, without pretense. (James 3:17)

What are the qualities of a really smart person? You might say: intelligence, a straight-A report card, a genius, a high IQ, someone in smart classes at school, someone who doesn't have to study, etc. The Bible is quick to separate earthly intelligence from spiritual wisdom. True wisdom has nothing to do with grades on a report card or what reading group you're in. Real wisdom is full of peace, full of mercy, full of good actions, and full of purity. Intelligence is formed in the mind, while wisdom is formed in the heart and then lived out in our lives. The only way to find true wisdom is to grow close to God. We all know people who claim to be super smart but who aren't loving or peaceful people. This is not wisdom. So the next time you might not feel very smart, just remember that real wisdom has everything to do with following Jesus, not your next math test score.

DAY 48

As Smart as You Are Kind

Who among you is wise and understanding? By his good conduct he should show that his works are done in the gentleness that comes from wisdom. (James 3:13)

Let whoever is wise pay attention to these things and consider the LORD's acts of faithful love. (Psalm 107:43)

There's nothing worse than a smart person who brags about being smart. In the world, some smart people may think they have the right to brag, to push other people around, and to feel important. According to God, however, the truly smart people are the ones who live good lives, lives that are full of love and gentleness towards others. The wiser you are, the more you help other people and the more you put yourself last. So the next time you make a good test score, it's okay to celebrate, but make sure you're also growing in the wisdom that really counts—godly wisdom. People might not remember what grades you make, but they will remember how you treat them.

DAY 49

Too Smart to Trick

Then we will no longer be little children, tossed by the waves and blown around by every wind of teaching, by human cunning with cleverness in the techniques of deceit. (Ephesians 4:14)

As children we're taught to believe everything adults tell us. If someone older than you tells you something, you can trust them, right? Sadly, this isn't always true. As a Christ follower you must measure everything people say with the Word of God. Just because your school teacher, coach, or favorite TV character teaches something doesn't mean it lines up with God's Word. That's why it's so important to know the Word of God for yourself. The Bible is always true, and you can always trust what it says. As girls, we have to be smart about what we believe. We have to know what we believe about Jesus so we can recognize a lie when it tries to trap us. Just because you're young doesn't mean you can't know truth. Study God's Word and it will protect you against the lies of the world.

DAY 50

Not Falling for That Again

The inexperienced one believes anything,
but the sensible one watches his steps. (Proverbs 14:15)

Have you ever had a really gullible friend? She believes anything and everything people tell her. If you told her a unicorn was following her, she'd turn around to check. It's funny until it comes to serious stuff. The Bible says that the simple man (or girl) believes anything he hears. Girls, it's time we grew up in our thinking. We cannot swallow every lie the world gives us. We have to watch our steps. There is a real enemy, the devil, trying to make us disobey God. We have to be smart. We must know the Word of God and hide it in our hearts so we can fight off the lies. Just because it's in our favorite TV show or movie doesn't make it right. Just because something seems to be right or feels right in our hearts doesn't make it right. It's all about what God's Word says is true. Seek God with all your heart, know the Bible, and quit believing everything you see, hear, or feel to be true in the world.

DAY 51

I Trust His Wisdom, Not My Own

Yes, God is exalted beyond our knowledge;
the number of his years cannot be counted. (Job 36:26)

Have you ever stood in a crowd of people taller than you? It's so annoying, especially if it happens at a concert or a parade. Then you have to depend on your parents to describe what's happening because your vision is limited.

The same thing happens in our lives every day. We have limited vision when it comes to our knowledge and understanding. We have to trust God's perspective of our problems and our blessings. He can see the whole picture of our lives and what He wants to accomplish in us. He knows what will bring us joy and what will bring us harm. Sometimes He leads us through something painful because He knows it will accomplish something good in us. Trust God's understanding, and don't rely on your own. He is wise, and He will lead you in the way you should go.

God's Promises

God gives us hundreds of promises in His Word, and He will honor every one. This section talks about several of those promises and the importance of believing God will keep them all.

DAY
52

We Have a Home in Heaven

"In my Father's house are many rooms; if not, I would have told you. I am going away to prepare a place for you. If I go away and prepare a place for you, I will come again and take you to myself, so that where I am you may be also." (John 14:2–3)

This world is not our home. Whenever bad things happen, it's great to remember that our forever home is in heaven. The home God is making for us is more beautiful and more glorious than anything we could imagine. When we know Jesus as Savior, we can cling to the promise of a future home with Him. He will never leave us, even through all eternity. God doesn't tell us a lot of detail about our future homes in heaven, but He tells us enough to know that it will be amazing. We know that His own hands will prepare it, and we know that we will be with Jesus. So be encouraged today that your heavenly Father loves you so much that He is building you a home in heaven where you will be with Him face-to-face forever.

DAY 53

We Will Be with Jesus Forever

Then we who are still alive, who are left, will be caught up together with them in the clouds to meet the Lord in the air, and so we will always be with the Lord. Therefore encourage one another with these words. (1 Thessalonians 4:17–18)

One of the greatest promises we have in Scripture is that we will spend eternity with Jesus. The Bible teaches that we will meet Jesus face-to-face and that we will always be with the Lord. No one really knows when this will happen or what it will be like, but God promises that it will happen. So no matter what you face today, know that your Savior loves you and will be with you forever. Scripture also says to "encourage one another with these words." Which one of your friends needs to be encouraged with this news? Maybe you know someone who has never heard the good news of Jesus. Let's lift our eyes off the problems in our lives and focus on Jesus. When you think about spending forever with Jesus, no struggle in the day is too tough to bear. He loves you so much.

DAY 54

We Have an Inheritance

"And everyone who has left houses or brothers or sisters or father or mother or children or fields because of my name will receive a hundred times more and will inherit eternal life." (Matthew 19:29)

Did you know that some people actually leave an inheritance to their pets when they die? There have been actual dogs, cats, and birds who have inherited thousands of dollars when their owners died. I'm not sure how many gold-plated doggie bowls Fido needs.

In Christ, we have a real live inheritance. It includes riches beyond anything we can possibly imagine. In Christ, you are a daughter of a king, and daughters of the king are always heiresses. Make no mistake, your Father is rich. He owns more than anyone on the earth. While we live on this earth, we do not seek worldly riches, but we seek heavenly riches like joy, peace, and forgiveness. We have value because Christ died for us on the cross and forever paid our ransom. But one day those riches will not be abstract; they will be real. Daughter of the King, live each day like your Father owns the whole world because He does. And you are His heiress.

DAY 55

Our Sins Are Forgiven

*"Come, let us settle this," says the L*ORD*. "Though your
sins are scarlet, they will be as white as snow; though
they are crimson red, they will be like wool." (Isaiah 1:18)*

There are some days that even the most beautiful girl feels ugly on the outside. Our hair won't look right; we feel weird in an outfit; we have a zit. It's nothing a ponytail, sweatpants, and a little makeup can't cure. But what about those days when we feel ugly on the inside? Sin—lying, bad words, disobeying, bad thoughts—covers our hearts and makes us spiritually ugly. Nothing we do can make it better. That's why Christ came. He alone has the cure for our sin. By His sacrifice on the cross, our sins are forgiven now and always. When Christ saves us, He forgives all our past, present, and future sins. He took our punishment on Himself. We no longer have to work at getting rid of our own sin. God does that for us. The next time you feel guilty over sin, remind yourself that you are forgiven by the blood of Christ on the cross. His sacrifice means you are forgiven now and always.

DAY 56

Nothing Will Separate You from the Love of God

For I am persuaded that neither death nor life, nor angels nor rulers, nor things present nor things to come, nor powers, nor height nor depth, nor any other created thing will be able to separate us from the love of God that is in Christ Jesus our Lord! (Romans 8:38–39)

Girl, this is a promise you need to write on your heart: your God loves you, and there is nothing you can do about it. His love is the strongest force in the universe. It will never break, never lessen, and never fall apart. God never gets over you. He loves you so much, He sent His own Son to die for you. His love circles you and protects you. It comforts you and brings you joy. Nothing is closer to you than the love of God. Nothing you do can separate you from it. Even the strongest earthly love sometimes cracks and shatters. Not God's love. He loves strong, loves completely, and loves forever. Your God will never fall out of love with you. Let the power of God's love sink into your heart. Let His love draw you in to know Him more. You are cherished by your Creator, and nothing can change that.

DAY 57

God Works Everything Together for Your Good

We know that all things work together for the good of those who love God, who are called according to his purpose. (Romans 8:28)

Have you ever taken something ugly or broken and made it into something useful? Sometimes a piece of junk in the right girl's hands can be transformed into something beautiful. That's exactly what God does for us. He takes all the broken parts of our day and works them together for our good. He brings learning from the pain. He strengthens our faith through the tears. When things are dark, He reveals His light the brightest. He paints, sews, glues, and knits the difficult times to reveal a beautiful masterpiece in our lives. The next time you face something tough, know that God is working all around you, even when you can't see it. The situation isn't good, but God knows how to bring something good from it. That's just how our Creator works.

DAY 58

We Have an Advocate for Our Sins

My little children, I am writing you these things so that you may not sin. But if anyone does sin, we have an advocate with the Father— Jesus Christ the righteous one. He himself is the atoning sacrifice for our sins, and not only for ours, but also for those of the whole world.
(1 John 2:1–2)

Has your mom ever had to talk to your teacher to get you out of trouble? Maybe you didn't do your homework because you were sick, or maybe you needed to leave class early to go on a trip. Without your mom, you'd get in big trouble. But because your mom goes before the teacher on your behalf, you don't get punished. That's exactly what Jesus does for us. Every time we sin we separate ourselves from God. Jesus advocates, or defends us, explaining that He took our sins when He went to the cross. He paid the price, so we no longer receive the punishment of being separated from God. Jesus loves you so much that He paid the price for your sins, and He continually serves as your Savior every single day.

The Heart of Faith

Anyone can talk the talk of faith in Christ, but a true Christian lives it out. This section focuses on becoming truly godly from the inside out.

DAY
59

You Can't Fake Obedience

Then Samuel said: Does the Lᴏʀᴅ take pleasure in burnt offerings and sacrifices as much as in obeying the Lᴏʀᴅ? Look: to obey is better than sacrifice, to pay attention is better than the fat of rams.
(1 Samuel 15:22)

Have you ever met a girl who seems spiritual, but she actually isn't? Maybe she sings worship songs to God on Sunday, but at school the next day she's mean to everyone and totally stuck up. This is not what God desires for us. He doesn't just want us to sing to Him or go through the motions of going to church. He wants our obedience. He wants our hearts. You can fake worship, but you can't fake obedience. If you are truly a follower of Christ, you will live how Jesus lived. You will honor God with your words, your thoughts, and your attitudes toward others. It matters that you obey God because that's how the world will come to know Him. So draw close to God. Worship Him with all your heart, but let that worship carry over to your actions. When you obey God, then He has your heart. That's what He wants most.

DAY 60

When No One Is Looking

*You supported me because of my integrity
and set me in your presence forever. (Psalm 41:12)*

Have your brothers or sisters ever treated you one way in front of your parents and another way when your parents weren't looking? It's easy to say and do the right thing when an adult is looking at you. But what about when you're by yourself? When you choose to do the right thing, even when no one is watching, that's called integrity. Even though your teachers or parents will never notice, God sees every good thing you do. There is no good act too big or too small that He does not notice. When you pick up that piece of trash, or make friends with a new student, or help your little sister with her homework, God sees, and it matters. So the next time you think no one sees you, so ahead and do the right thing anyway. God will use your integrity to encourage others and draw you closer to Him.

DAY 61

She Thinks She Can Sing

In the same way faith, if it doesn't have works,
is dead by itself. (James 2:17)

We all have a friend who thinks she can sing. She talks about singing all day, she plays music in her car, but when she actually steps up to the microphone, everyone wants to run and hide. You can talk about singing, but unless you have a pretty voice, you're not a singer. It's the same way with faith. You can talk about God all day long. You can go to church and claim to know Bible verses. But if your life doesn't match your words, then you don't actually have faith at all. True faith always has actions to back it up. Faith produces fruit in your life like love, patience, self-control, and gentleness. If you don't have any fruit, then you're not alive in Christ. We don't work to save ourselves, but once we come to Christ, we will have good works. His love is always powerful enough to change us. When you're captured by the love of Christ, He will change you from the inside out.

DAY 62

Accidentally an Athlete

Do what you have learned and received and heard from me and seen in me, and the God of peace will be with you. (Philippians 4:9)

Nobody learns to dance by reading a big book on ballet. You can't Google "softball" and learn how to pitch. Books might give you clues on how to be better, but they can't give you the skills. You learn to dance by taking lessons. You learn to pitch a softball by throwing the ball over and over until you get it right. The same is true in Christ. God's Word teaches us what we need to know, but we have to actually live it out for it to make a difference. We have to practice love, forgiveness, kind words, and trust. Reading about it doesn't mean we've lived it. The more knowledge you have doesn't make you more godly unless you're actually using the things you've learned. Study the Bible, listen to wise people, but put what you learn into practice. The more you practice, the better you get and the more your life will look like the life of Christ.

DAY 63

I'm Wide-Awake

Be alert, stand firm in the faith, be courageous, be strong.
Do everything in love. (1 Corinthians 16:13–14)

Have you ever messed with one of your friends while she was sleeping? Maybe you put shaving cream on her face or drew on her with a marker. It's easy to play jokes on someone when she's sleeping because she's in her own world. While your friend dreams of Prince Charming, you're covering her hair with stickers. She can't fight back because she has no idea what's happening. It's the same with our faith in Christ. The Bible tells us to "be alert." That means we're to be wide-awake in Christ. We must learn how to recognize the enemy's attacks. When he tries to get us to lie, gossip, or talk badly to our siblings, we know it's a trap. When you're wide-awake, you can stop an attack. Stay alert in your walk with God. Pray, worship Him, and read the Bible. Choose to live out your faith to make it real. When you're wide-awake, no one can try to convince you to do something that's wrong.

DAY 64

Believe Big Things

*Jesus answered them, "Truly I tell you, if you have faith
and do not doubt, you will not only do what was done
to the fig tree, but even if you tell this mountain, 'Be lifted up
and thrown into the sea,' it will be done." (Matthew 21:21)*

Faith is your confidence in Christ, even when you can't see Him. Some girls claim to follow Christ, but their faith is small. They might believe Jesus can save them, but they don't believe He can help with bad habits. Some girls have big faith, trusting God enough to live for Him, even when it's hard. Jesus said that strong faith is enough to make a mountain fall into the ocean. Jesus didn't mean we should pray for crazy things just to see if they'd happen. He meant that we should live our lives with big faith. God delights to show Himself strong. He wants to help you accomplish great things for Him. Even if you only have a little faith, God can work. But imagine if you believed God for big things. When you stay close to Him, know His Word, and live out your faith, He will show up. It won't always be the way you expected, but it will be exactly what you need. Believe Him.

DAY 65

Real Faith, Real Justice

*"Learn to do what is good. Pursue justice.
Correct the oppressor. Defend the rights of the fatherless.
Plead the widow's cause." (Isaiah 1:17)*

Although the Bible gives us clear guidelines for living, it doesn't necessarily answer every single thing about our personal lives. It doesn't tell you if your exact outfit is okay to wear. It doesn't tell you if the movie you saw last weekend was really good to watch. Some things are confusing; that's why you need to spend time in prayer and with your parents to learn God's will. But some things are crystal clear. God always wants us to take care of the poor people around us. The Bible says that God has a heart for the fatherless and the widow. He loves the orphans and the elderly, people who can't take care of themselves. When you have a heart for God, you will have a heart to defend the weak. In your world, that might be a kid in your class who has special needs. It might be an elderly lady in your neighborhood who could use a friend. You don't have to ask God if He wants you to look out for these people; He always does. When you show love to the weak, you are showing love to God and bring Him glory.

DAY 66

Castle on the Rock

*"Therefore, everyone who hears these words of mine and acts
on them will be like a wise man who built his house on the rock."
(Matthew 7:24)*

Building sand castles on the beach is fun. You use buckets and shovels to make the castle, decorate it with shells, and try to keep your little siblings from knocking it down. When you come back to the beach next year, you don't expect your same sand castle to still be there. That's because sand castles don't last. The slightest ocean wave will rip it to pieces. That's why Jesus tells us to build our house on the rock and not the sand. When we listen to the words of Christ and put them into action, we build our foundation on rocks. That's real faith. Then when the winds of pain and trials blow, our faith doesn't crumble; it stands strong. But when we listen to the Words of God, but don't obey Him, we build our faith on sand. When the first hard thing comes along, we crumble. We're easily shaken and easily depressed. Where are you building your house? Build on the rock of God. Listen to Him and obey His words. Stay close to God and do what He says. The winds of the world will not be able to shake you.

Already Famous

The power of the spotlight is strong. At some point, every girl dreams of being discovered, standing on stage, and being famous. This section focuses on sacrificing our own dreams of fame in order to seek the fame of God.

DAY
67

Center Stage

Yes, LORD, we wait for you in the path of your judgments.
Our desire is for your name and renown. (Isaiah 26:8)

What famous person most gets on your nerves? You don't like their music or movies, and you wonder why they are even famous in the first place. The world craves fame. They want someone to worship and admire, someone to photograph, and someone who's life looks better than theirs. There is only one who is worthy of fame, the Lord. He alone deserves our worship and our constant focus and admiration. Some girls spend their lives trying to get discovered so they can be famous. The only fame worth pursuing is the fame of the Lord. When you dedicate yourself to making Him famous in the world, you experience true joy and purpose—something the fame of the world will never give you.

DAY 68

Not Meant to Be Worshipped

Whatever you do, in word or in deed, do everything in the name of the Lord Jesus, giving thanks to God the Father through him.
(Colossians 3:17)

Several popular TV shows are dedicated to helping people become famous. Whether it's through singing, dancing, acting, or even a popular YouTube video, it's so tempting to seek our own fame. In Christ, we don't seek our own fame; we seek the fame of God. We want His name to be glorified in the earth, not our own name. In fact, we want the presence of God to swallow up our life so that we disappear inside it. Spend your life making God famous, not yourself. Speak His name more than your own and work hard to make Him known. The more you seek your own fame, the more miserable you'll be, but seeking the fame of God leads to our joy. Make Him famous.

DAY 69

His Dream for You

"Go, therefore, and make disciples of all nations, baptizing them in the name of the Father and of the Son and of the Holy Spirit, teaching them to observe everything I have commanded you. And remember, I am with you always, to the end of the age." (Matthew 28:19–20)

Did you know that God has big dreams for you? He wants to use you in ways you can't even imagine. Unlike the world's selfish dreams, His dreams are all about helping you make Him famous. In Matthew, Jesus teaches His disciples to go into every nation and make more disciples. He tells them to teach His words and to baptize those who believe. Wherever we go or whatever we become in this life, our job is the same as the disciples who first heard Jesus' words. We are to share the words of Christ with everyone who will listen. We are to go into our schools, our families, our communities, and our world teaching about Christ. Maybe you can't hop on a plane to China, but you have lost people all around you who need to hear the gospel. God's dream for you is that you would spend your life worshipping Him and inviting other people to come to Christ. That is the greatest dream you could ever have, and when you stay in His presence, it will come true.

DAY 70

Old Famous People

All flesh is like grass, and all its glory like a flower of the grass. The grass withers, and the flower falls, but the word of the Lord endures forever. And this word is the gospel that was proclaimed to you.
(1 Peter 1:24–25)

Quick—think of a famous movie star from the 1970s.

Out of the hundreds of famous movies made in that decade, could you even name one person? Two people? That's probably because you don't really care about people who were famous nearly fifty years ago. You know people who are famous right now. Fame is short. Even if you become really famous, adored by the media, and popular to everyone, in a few short years, no one will remember your name. The world's worship never lasts very long. Only the fame of Christ lasts forever. The Bible says that our glory as humans fades away like the grass. But the Word of the Lord lives forever. When you spend your life making God famous, worshiping Him, and telling others about Him, you wrap yourself up in a story that will never die. His fame will never end. The world will never forget the name of Jesus. Make God famous with your life. That's the only fame that matters.

DAY 71

What Are You Famous For?

The news about him spread even more, and large crowds would come together to hear him and to be healed of their sicknesses.
(Luke 5:15)

Everyone is known for something. Some girls are known because they have a powerful singing voice. Some girls are famous because they posted an awesome YouTube video. Some girls are popular just because they're pretty. Some girls are "famous" for bad reasons—they're known for their bad temper or tendency to be a drama queen. Jesus was famous too—not because He was rich or talented. He was famous for preaching the Word of God and for healing sick people. Jesus attracted the poor and the sick with His words of love and hope. The Bible says that large crowds of people followed Him. What are you known for? Are you recognized by your talents alone? Do people know you because of your looks or your bad temper? Instead of seeking fame for selfish reasons, start loving the outcasts. Be known for your loving spirit. When you seek God and live out His love for other people, you will become known. God will draw people to you so they can know more about Him. Everyone is famous for something. Be famous for acting, speaking, and thinking like Jesus so He will be famous in you.

True Love

True love is something every girl longs to experience. This section talks about the only place to find real love and how to recognize fake loves that try to steal your heart.

DAY
72

True Love Is Patient

Love is patient, love is kind. Love does not envy, is not boastful, is not arrogant. (1 Corinthians 13:4)

Movies and fairy tales teach us that love rushes in, that when two people love each other, they get together immediately. This isn't love. Real love is patient. It doesn't rush, and it doesn't get in a hurry. It doesn't demand "right now," but it waits on the other person. God is so patient with us. He never pushes us or hurries us into a relationship with Him. He wants us to come to Him with our whole hearts, but He waits until we do. True love never violates God's design for purity. It patiently waits for God's timing and obeys God's boundaries. If anyone claims to love you, but does not patiently follow the Word of God, that love is a lie. Be patient for real love. It is worth waiting for.

DAY 73

True Love Is Not Boastful or Conceited

Love is patient, love is kind. Love does not envy, is not boastful, is not arrogant. (1 Corinthians 13:4)

Have you ever had a friend who's glued to a mirror? She constantly checks her hair and makeup, and she always talks about herself. She'll listen to you as long as you talk about her. This is the opposite of love. Love isn't eager to be in the spotlight. It doesn't constantly brag about accomplishments. Love doesn't need to remind everyone how great it is all the time. We find this love in Christ. Jesus was the picture of humility. His entire life was about serving others, healing others, listening to others, even sacrificing Himself for us. When you truly love someone, you don't need to brag or be arrogant around them. Instead, serve them and talk about yourself last. In a world that's full of pride, a humble love will be the most refreshing kind of love.

DAY 74

True Love Is Not Self-Seeking or Easily Angered

[Love] is not rude, is not self-seeking, is not irritable,
and does not keep a record of wrongs. (1 Corinthians 13:5)

Have you ever seen a dating couple who fights all the time? It's annoying to everyone around them. The Bible says that true love isn't easily angered. True love doesn't fly off the handle or get easily frustrated. Instead, it's kind and patient. True love gives grace and overlooks offenses. That's how God treats us. He has patience with us and gives us grace. He's quick to forgive and slow to get angry. So if you see a couple constantly fighting, you know that they don't understand true love at all. True love chooses grace over anger.

DAY 75

No Record of Wrongs

[Love] is not rude, is not self-seeking, is not irritable, and does not keep a record of wrongs. (1 Corinthians 13:5)

Teachers usually have a system of tracking behavior. If you have your homework and good behavior for several days, you get a reward. If you goof off and get in trouble, they keep track of that too. Too many bad reports will get you in big trouble. Did you know that God doesn't keep count of your mistakes? When you mess up, He doesn't write it down or put a check mark by your name. That's because true love keeps no record of wrongs. He never throws your past mistakes in your face. We love this about God, but sometimes it's hard to love other people like this. But if we really love someone, we don't keep count of the times they hurt our feelings. We don't drag up stuff from the past to make them feel bad. True love forgives and overlooks mistakes.

DAY 76

Written on His Hands

*"Look, I have inscribed you on the palms of my hands;
your walls are continually before me." (Isaiah 49:16)*

When you need to write something down really fast but you don't have any paper, what do you do? You write it on your hand. Almost every girl does it. Did you know that God has something written on His hands too? In Isaiah, God says that His people are written on His hands. And you don't forget something written on your hands. You are so important to God, it's as if your very name was tattooed on His hands. You are constantly on His mind and in His thoughts. This verse also reminds us of the hands of Christ. The scars in His hands continually point to His love for you. He does not forget you. You never have to beg for His attention because you always have it. Respond to God's love for you by loving Him back.

DAY 77

Obedience from the Heart

The Lord said: "These people approach me with their speeches to honor me with lip-service—yet their hearts are far from me, and human rules direct their worship of me." (Isaiah 29:13)

You probably aren't in love with your math homework. You don't write songs about math, sleep with your math book under your pillow, or throw math-themed birthday parties. You do your math homework because you want to make a good grade, pass your test, and because your parents make you. That's how some people follow God. They do the right things because they have to, because it's what God tells them to do, but they have no love for God and no joy in His presence. God hates this kind of obedience. More than He wants our empty good works, He wants our hearts. He wants you to fall in love with Him so you get joy from obeying Him. He wants to make you happy and to bless you. Worship God because you love Him. True love for God produces obedience that brings joy.

DAY 78

Anybody Out There?

The LORD looks down from heaven on the human race to see if there is one who is wise, one who seeks God. (Psalm 14:2)

God is searching for girls who are wise. He's looking to see if anyone will love Him enough to obey Him, even when it's hard. Most girls chase after their own desires rather than the Lord's. They seek beauty and popularity and have no heart for God or love for others. True wisdom is rare and precious, and only a few girls will find it. Seek after the Lord with your whole heart. Become the wise girl God is searching for. Run after the Lord and dare to obey Him, even when it costs you something.

DAY 79

The Worst Husband Ever

Serve the Lord with gladness; come before him with joyful songs.
(Psalm 100:2)

Things you don't want to hear from your future husband: "I guess I'll talk to you since I'm your husband and I have to." "Here's your birthday present. I had to get you one since we're married." "Married people are supposed to live together, so I guess we can share the same house."

How would you feel if you married this loser? You'd be miserable. He did all the right things, buying gifts, listening, sharing a house, but he had no joy doing it. That's not love. Just doing the right things isn't enough. It's your heart that matters. That's how it is in our walk with God. God wants to give us joy as we obey Him. In fact, He wants you to be in love with Him, so you obey Him out of joy and not out of obligation. When you serve Him with a gloomy face, it doesn't please God. Where do we get this joy to obey God? He gives it to us. When you spend time in God's presence, you will be joyful. God delights to fill your heart with love for Him. So remember that God doesn't want gloom obedience; He wants your whole heart. When you love Him first, joy will always follow.

DAY 80

Hosea's Love Story

Then the L<small>ORD</small> said to me, "Go again; show love to a woman who is loved by another man and is an adulteress, just as the L<small>ORD</small> loves the Israelites though they turn to other gods and love raisin cakes."
(Hosea 3:1)

Every great story has a great villain—someone we love to hate, usually an evil witch or wizard with a bad temper. There's also a beautiful princess and a prince who must rescue her. In our love story with God, we are the ones who need rescuing, but we're not beautiful. We are full of sin, covered in the filth of selfishness, pride, and greed. In fact, we look a lot more like the villain than the innocent victim. In the story of Hosea, God calls Hosea to marry a woman who cheats on him. Every time she cheats, Hosea keeps taking her back. He keeps loving her even when she doesn't deserve it. That's what God does to us. Even when we are ugly and unlovable, He rescues us—not as a beautiful princess, but as a nasty, sinful villain. He loves us so much that He sees beyond our sin. He loves us enough to rescue us, and He loves us enough to change us. Has God rescued you? Then He will make you beautiful. He will make you into the princess you were meant to be. Let Him save you, then let Him change you. It will be the greatest love story of your life.

DAY 81

Adopted

He predestined us to be adopted as sons through Jesus Christ for himself, according to the good pleasure of his will, to the praise of his glorious grace that he lavished on us in the Beloved One.
(Ephesians 1:5–6)

Have you ever been around a family with adopted children? No matter the color, gender, or age, adopted children belong to their parents as much as any biological child. Adoptive parents love their children and consider them fully their sons and daughters. Did you know that we are all adopted in Christ? We were separated from God by our sin. Through Christ's work on the cross, God adopted us into His family. We were born into sin, but adopted into salvation. Like adopted children, God loves us more than we could imagine, just like we were His natural children. He also promises us an inheritance and blessings. We are part of the family of God, not born into it, but adopted through our faith in Christ. Our adoption was expensive; it cost the blood of Christ. But to God, you are worth that sacrifice. True love is being adopted by your Father.

DAY 82

Your First Love

We love because he first loved us. (1 John 4:19)

When you were born, your parents absolutely fell in love with you. They loved you because the day you came home from the hospital, you immediately stood up and started cleaning the house. Um, no. In your first days of life, you didn't do anything for your parents except cry, sleep, and dirty your diaper. You were expensive, painful to bring into the world, and a LOT of hard work. But they fell in love with you anyway because you're their daughter. That's exactly how God is with us. He loves you so much just because He made you. Before you could ever do anything good for God, He loved you. Before you reached out to Him, He knew you. His love always comes first. You love Him because He loved you. Rest in the confidence that your God is crazy about you, not because of what you do for Him, but because of who you are to Him.

DAY 83

True Love Rules

See what great love the Father has given us that
we should be called God's children—and we are! (1 John 3:1)

Every girl wants to be loved. We want someone to love us totally and completely for who we are. Music, fairy tales, and movies offer a lot of definitions for true love: butterflies in your stomach, heart beating fast, forever promises. Sadly, we've seen a lot of relationships fall apart that claimed to start with love. The Bible gives us a real picture of true love, the greatest love you could ever experience. Jesus laid down His life for you. He loved you so much that He took your punishment for sin even though He was innocent. There is no greater love. This is love that cannot be broken. It will never fade. Whenever you wonder if anyone loves you, think of Christ's love for you. It is the greatest, most powerful love that covers you completely.

Tough Questions for God

God isn't afraid of our questions. In fact, asking tough questions can help you know more about God and more about yourself. This section addresses some of the tough questions girls ask God.

DAY 84

What If God Can't Hear Me?

I love those who love me, and those who search for me find me.
(Proverbs 8:17)

Have you ever prayed and felt like God couldn't hear you? Or maybe you asked Him for something that never happened. No matter how you feel, you can be confident that God hears every sound of your voice. He knows you, and He is listening. In fact, God hears more than any person on the earth. He not only hears your words, but He knows your heart and what you're really asking. He also knows what you need better than you know yourself because He made you and He saved you. So trust that He can hear you and wants to hear you. Trust that He still loves you more than you could imagine. Go to the Bible to hear His voice—you will always find it there. Search for God and you will find Him.

DAY 85

What If I Don't Feel Close to God?

Draw near to God, and he will draw near to you. Cleanse your hands, sinners, and purify your hearts, you double-minded. (James 4:8)

Sometimes you just don't feel close to God. Maybe you had a bad day or you just feel alone. Everyone feels this way sometimes. The best thing to do when you feel far from God is to look at the words of God in the Bible. Then you can trust what He says and not rely on your own feelings, which can deceive you. Scripture says when you draw near to God, He will draw near to you. That means no matter where you are or what you've done, He will come close to you when you draw near to Him. He loves you so much that He gave His own Son to die in your place. Of course He will take the time to come close to you when you need Him. So no matter how you feel, know that God will come near to you when you come near to Him.

DAY 86

Does God Still Do Miracles?

LORD, I have heard the report about you; LORD, I stand in awe of your deeds. Revive your work in these years; make it known in these years. In your wrath remember mercy! (Habakkuk 3:2)

God loves us to ask Him to do big things in our lives. He loves to accomplish things we never thought were possible. When you have big faith in God, you believe that He really could do the impossible. In this verse, Habakkuk cries out to God. He says that he's heard of the things God has done in the past and he asks God to do those big things again. At some point, many adults stop asking God to do big things. Maybe they lose faith or get stuck in the ordinary. You don't have to have an ordinary faith because your God is not ordinary. Ask Him to do miracles. Ask Him to save someone you love. Ask Him to heal. Ask Him to break down the walls in your family. Dare to believe He will do it. Many times He will. If He doesn't seem to answer, it may be that He is saying "no" or "not now," but God never fails to hear and answer. Stand in awe of the Lord. Remember how big He is and never be afraid to ask Him to do big things for you.

DAY 87

What Is Heaven Like?

"In my Father's house are many rooms; if not, I would have told you. I am going away to prepare a place for you. If I go away and prepare a place for you, I will come again and receive you to myself, so that where I am you may be also." (John 14:2–3)

Then the one seated on the throne said, "Look, I am making everything new." He also said, "Write, because these words are faithful and true." (Revelation 21:5)

Wouldn't it be great if God included a picture of heaven in the Bible? Couldn't He just get down in the dirt—Jesus drew in the dirt, right?—and give us a quick sketch of our forever home and upload it to Instagram? He didn't. Maybe we don't know much about heaven because God wants us to desire Him more than the riches that wait for us. God did write enough about heaven to let us know it's going to be awesome. No, we won't be angels and we won't play harps. And God invented the rainbow, so you know we're not going to be wearing white all the time (huge sigh of relief from those of us who need a little color). Heaven will be an actual place. There will be no suffering and no crying. It will have riches beyond our imaginations, and we will reign with Christ as royalty. Above all we will see our Savior face-to-face. Be encouraged that God's love for His children is great, and one day we will be with Him forever if we know Christ as our Savior.

DAY 88

Who Made God?

"I am the Alpha and the Omega," says the Lord God, "the one who is, who was, and who is coming, the Almighty." (Revelation 1:8)

Before the mountains were born, before you gave birth to the earth and the world, from eternity to eternity, you are God. (Psalm 90:2)

No one made God. He was not born, created, or designed. He is older than the earth, the sun, and every universe in every solar system. The Bible says God is from eternity to eternity. It's hard to imagine something lasting forever. Our human minds can't understand it. But we can trust that God will last forever. He had no beginning, and He had no end. It also means that God's love for you will never come to an end. Your God is huge, bigger than every problem you could ever face, bigger than all evil. He is the same yesterday, today, and forever. Worship Him with your whole heart.

DAY 89

What Is the Trinity?

The grace of the Lord Jesus Christ, and the love of God, and the fellowship of the Holy Spirit be with you all. (2 Corinthians 13:13)

God said, "Let us make man in our image, according to our likeness." (Genesis 1:26)

*T*hree gods in one? That sounds a little weird. Is that like when my cell phone is also my computer, my alarm, and my calculator? Not exactly. God exists as three people at the same time. He is fully God the Father, fully Jesus, and fully the Holy Spirit. It's hard to understand with earthly minds. God doesn't choose who He wants to be that day; He is all three persons, three in one, all the time. Although Jesus was completely human on the earth, He was also fully God. In the same way, when you know Christ, you have the Holy Spirit—the very person of God living inside you. The Holy Spirit encourages you, counsels you, and convicts you when you sin. Again, it's really complicated, so if you don't understand, don't stress out. The more you walk with God, the more it will become clear. You can trust God the Father, Jesus, and the Holy Spirit to work in your life for your salvation and your good.

Guard Your Heart

Your heart is the most precious thing you have. Every day you have opportunities to give your heart away to someone or something that will treat it badly. This section deals with letting God have your whole heart because His love for you is real.

DAY
90

Secret Keeper

I will say concerning the Lord, who is my refuge and my fortress, my God in whom I trust. (Psalm 91:2)

When was the last time a friend blurted out your secret? It's a horrible feeling to find out someone is untrustworthy. The Bible says that God is a fortress we can trust. We have to be very careful whom we entrust with our secrets. Start by trusting God. You can tell Him everything because He already knows. He's also the only one you can trust who can actually do something about your problems. He can help you through and give you courage and peace in every situation. Sometimes people don't really want to help; they just want to know your secrets. God isn't like that. He always wants to help, and He is always trustworthy to listen and to guide you through.

DAY 91

Lockdown

Guard your heart above all else,
for it is the source of life. (Proverbs 4:23)

Has your school ever had a lock down? Even a practice drill can be a little scary, when the teacher locks the doors and students assume an emergency position. We have lock downs to protect us from people who want to hurt us or people who try to get in but really don't need to be there. God asks us to put a kind of lock down on our hearts as well. That doesn't mean that we block people out; it just means we use caution when giving our hearts away. Scripture calls our heart "the source of life." Too many girls give their hearts away to guys too easily. They have no lock and no protection around their "source of life." What kind of lock do you have on your heart? Do you give your heart to anyone, or do you show caution? Instead of falling for every guy, guard your heart. Let God, your parents, and godly mentors help. Your heart is the most precious thing you have. Guard it like the treasure it is.

DAY 92

The One Who Holds Your Heart

Trust in him at all times, you people; pour out your hearts before him. God is our refuge. Selah. (Psalm 62:8)

A lot of people will try to steal your heart. They will promise you things and say words that seem right at the time. The only one you can always trust, always run to, and always believe is God. We can pour out our whole hearts to Him because He is our refuge. He is our safe place, our trusted shelter. He made us and knows us. He is worthy of our hearts, but He doesn't force your heart from you. If you haven't quite trusted God with your whole heart, dare to trust Him now. Put all your fears, all your dreams, and all your insecurities on Him. He will prove trustworthy.

DAY 93

When Your Heart Is Broken

The LORD is near the brokenhearted;
he saves those crushed in spirit. (Psalm 34:18)

Have you ever accidentally dropped a piece of glass? It doesn't crack neatly into equal parts; it shatters into thousands of tiny pieces. If you've ever had your heart broken, you know that it feels just like the shattering of that glass—like there's no way anyone is putting this thing back together. When someone you trusted betrays you and breaks your heart, there is only one place to run—straight into the arms of God. The Bible says that God is close to the brokenhearted. He knows what you're feeling and what you need. He sees each and every piece of your heart, and He is the only one who can put it back together. Hold out your broken heart to the Lord, and He will heal it completely.

The Waiting Game

Nobody likes to wait. It's stressful, annoying, and sometimes scary. No matter what you're waiting on, you can trust God to give you the strength to trust Him.

DAY
94

In the Waiting Room

Be silent before the LORD and wait expectantly for him;
do not be agitated by one who prospers in his way,
by the person who carries out evil plans. (Psalm 37:7)

Waiting is the worst. We wait every single day. We wait in the lunch line, wait to check out at the store, and wait for our sisters to get ready in the morning. It's miserable. Sometimes it's more serious, like waiting to hear if a grandparent has a disease or waiting to see if your dad gets to keep his job. In this life, we will always be waiting for something. Unlike the world, we don't have to wait full of fear and stress. We have hope. God offers promises to us in His Word. He will never leave us. He works things together for our good. When we wait on the Lord, we can wait with hope and courage. What are you waiting for? Take it to the Lord and know that it is important to Him.

DAY 95

Trust in the Wait

Therefore, brothers and sisters, be patient until the Lord's coming. See how the farmer waits for the precious fruit of the earth and is patient with it until it receives the early and the late rains. You also must be patient. Strengthen your hearts, because the Lord's coming is near. (James 5:7–8)

Have you ever tried to grow a vegetable or a flower? You till the ground, dig a little hole, bury the seed, and water it. Then what? You wait. Hours and days will pass, and it looks like nothing is happening. You keep checking and keep watering, but still nothing. Then suddenly you see a little sprout. The most important part of that seed's growth happened under the surface, in the wait. That's just like us. While we're waiting for something to happen, God is able to grow us closer to Him. Beneath the surface, in our character, God is always working. Even when we can't see it, He's changing us, working on us to look more like Him. So the next time you can't see what God is doing or you're waiting for something to happen, just remember God is always at work. It just might be happening below the surface.

DAY 96

Growing While We Wait

And not only that, but we also rejoice in our afflictions, because we know that affliction produces endurance, endurance produces proven character, and proven character produces hope. (Romans 5:3–4)

Nobody understands pain like a piñata. There it is, filled with candy, gently swinging from a tree, when all of a sudden it's assaulted with sticks. Greedy kids pound the piñata until candy falls from the sky. The fact is, unless you crush the piñata, you can't get the candy. Sometimes it can feel like life is beating you up. Whatever pain you face, you can be confident God has a plan to use it. God never lets us go through something hard unless something good will eventually come out of it. Romans says that our afflictions, or our pain, produces good qualities in us. The more we're crushed down, the more beautiful we are and the stronger we become.

DAY 97

Waiting on Everyday Things

Trust in the LORD with all your heart, and do not rely on your own understanding; in all your ways know him, and he will make your paths straight. (Proverbs 3:5–6)

Sometimes waiting with joy means you need an attitude adjustment. When you "trust in the LORD with all your heart," you can have patience in waiting, especially in everyday life. When your mom needs to run to the store, or you have to wait an extra day to do something fun, you don't whine or complain. You trust God and you stay happy. The next time you feel yourself starting to get frustrated with waiting, ask God to give you His perspective and His patience. Sometimes the best way to serve your parents is just by having a good attitude if you have to wait for something you want. It's hard, but it's possible in Christ.

Bad Hair Days

Whether it's beautifully styled or a rat's nest, a girl's hair says everything about her mood. This section is a funny way of looking at our bad days through the hair styles we choose. Straight or curly, frizzy or smooth, every strand matters to God.

DAY
98

The Ombre Day: Starts Out Good, Then Changes to Bad

Don't worry about anything, but in everything, through prayer and petition with thanksgiving, present your requests to God. (Philippians 4:6)

Ombre is a pretty popular, cute hair style where your hair is one color on top and gradually turns to a different color on the bottom. It can also be used to describe a crazy day. Have you ever had a day that starts out happy and normal, but then something happens that totally changes the way things were going? I call this an ombre day. Sometimes you think things are going great, but then you get hit with a totally different kind of day than you started out with. Before you freak out too much, know that this surprise twist in your day is not a shock to God. God's Word says that the peace of God will guard your heart and your mind. The next time an ombre day sneaks up on you, take it to God and He will make something beautiful out of your two-toned day.

DAY 99

The French Braid Day: Twisted Up and Overwhelmed

> *Consider it a great joy, my brothers and sisters, whenever you experience various trials, because you know that the testing of your faith produces endurance. (James 1:2–3)*

Sometimes you have one of those days that's kind of like a french braid—thick and twisted. Maybe you have too much homework. Maybe your parents' expectations are piling up. Or maybe you're having friend problems. Whatever the reason for stress, God is on your side. He wants to give you wisdom and peace to get through it. God's Word promises that when our faith is tested, it produces perseverance. Every time you trust God in the middle of something hard, your faith is strengthened. It's like a workout for your faith. You get stronger in who God made you to be. So the next time you feel a little like a super-tight braid that raises your eyebrows, ask God to fill you with peace. He will help you through and grow your faith in the process.

we are going through a lot. we
need to count it all joy though.
He put these trials here for us.

The Side Ponytail Day:
Feeling Off-Center

Set your minds on things above,
not on earthly things. (Colossians 3:2)

Sometimes you have just an all-around weird day, I call it a side pony-tail day, where everything seems off-center. Maybe your mom was in a bad mood and your easy teacher suddenly gives you tons of work. It's just one of those days. Well, everyday, but especially on these weird days, it's important to set our eyes on the Lord, not on earthly things. What we can see with our eyes isn't always the whole story. God knows what you need, and He can give you strength to deal with anything that comes your way. Prepare in advance that you won't be discouraged on days like this but that you will give your day to the Lord. He is fully capable of keeping you focused, even on a side ponytail day.

DAY 101

The Highlights Day: Bright on Top, but Dark Underneath

The Lord said: These people approach me with their speeches to honor me with lip-service—yet their hearts are far from me, and human rules direct their worship of me. (Isaiah 29:13)

Highlights are a fun way of lightening up your hair. Partial highlights are a quicker, cheaper option that lighten the top layer of hair—making it look colored all the way through—but it's actually still dark underneath. Sometimes we have days that are like partial highlights; we act sunny and happy on the outside, but inside we feel yucky. It's exhausting to act one way and feel another, plus most people aren't fooled by a fake smile. Bring these feelings to God and ask Him to give you real joy, peace, and love. He is able to transform you from the inside out, so that every smile is genuine and every kind word is heartfelt. Let Him make you one color, through and through.

DAY 102

The Bed-Head Day: I Just Want to Stay Asleep

I complain and groan morning, noon, and night, and he hears my voice. (Psalm 55:17)

Sometimes we just want to crawl under the covers and stay there all day. When you have one of those days, know that God hasn't forgotten about you. He knows your deepest emotions and the things that caused them. Instead of hiding away, face the day head-on with the God of the universe at your side. The Bible says He hears your voice when you call to Him. He will never leave your side, and He will help you get through the day. In His presence, you can have joy, peace, and love, even in the middle of a bed-head day.

DAY 103

The Perfect Hair Day: Please Don't Touch

This is the day the LORD has made;
let us rejoice and be glad in it. (Psalm 118:24)

Some days are just perfect. We get along with everyone, we make godly decisions, and everything goes our way. Praise God! God wants to draw close to you in your joy as well as in your pain. Invite God to celebrate with you when you have a great day because it was a gift from Him. Thank Him for His blessings. Recognize His presence in the day. Sing worship songs of praise to Him. He is delighted to bless you with a good day because you are His daughter. Never let a good day go unnoticed, and don't forget to invite God into the great day He made especially for you.

Share Your Faith

We have a story the world needs to hear. This section focuses on empowering you to share the gospel with your friends with boldness and to realize it's all about God.

DAY
104

Every Opportunity

Act wisely toward outsiders, making the most of the time.
(Colossians 4:5)

Sharing your faith doesn't just have to happen on a mission trip or at church. In fact, the best environment for telling someone about Jesus might just be the soccer field, or the gymnastics studio, or in the band room. God wants to use your talents and hobbies as a way to reach out to people who don't know Him. Every place you go and everything you do can present the chance to talk about Jesus. You just have to be yourself and open your eyes to the opportunities. What do you love to do? The next time you're doing it, look around to see who might need to hear the good news of Jesus.

DAY 105

Shake the Dust from Your Feet

"If any place does not welcome you or listen to you, when you leave there, shake the dust off your feet as a testimony against them."
(Mark 6:11)

Have you ever desperately wanted someone to come to faith in Christ? Maybe you've tried talking to him about Jesus and showing him your changed life. Maybe you've shared your testimony and taken him or her to church. In the Bible, Jesus told His disciples to shake the dust from their feet whenever they met someone who refused to welcome them and accept the gospel. When Jesus said this, He didn't mean we suddenly reject that person or be rude to them. He just meant we can't let their refusal of Christ weigh us down. We can't control a person's reaction to the gospel; we can only share. Also, be encouraged. You never know how God is working under the surface of that person's life, even when you can't see it. So share the gospel, and if people don't want to hear it, let them refuse. In a few weeks, they may be ready to hear the truth again.

DAY 106

Your Story Matters

Come and listen, all who fear God,
and I will tell what he has done for me. (Psalm 66:16)

Now many Samaritans from that town believed in him
because of what the woman said when she testified,
"He told me everything I ever did." (John 4:39)

It can be scary to share your faith with someone who doesn't know Christ. One of the best ways to start is to just tell your own story, called a testimony. If you are a Christian, you have a story of how God came into your life and saved you. It might not be a glamorous story in your opinion, but it's your story and it's the most important one. Nobody knows your story like you do. So the next time you want to share your faith but don't know what to say, just start with "Let me tell you what God has done in my life." It might be just what your friend needs to hear.

DAY 107

When You're Different

"You are blessed when they insult you and persecute you and falsely say every kind of evil against you because of me." (Matthew 5:11)

If you really walk with God, sometimes people are going to be mean to you. They might not understand why you won't watch bad movies, say bad words, or cheat on a test. They might make fun of what you wear. This is hurtful, but you can be encouraged that God told us this would happen. When you are teased because you're different, God takes this very personally. He even called you "blessed." I don't know about you, but it sure doesn't seem very blessed to be teased. The truth is that you're blessed because you have the very presence of God in your life. You are not a slave to the world. You have true joy, true peace, and true happiness that no amount of teasing can take away. You're blessed because you don't blend in with the world, and it shows.

DAY 108

When You Mess Up

For all have sinned and fall short of the glory of God. (Romans 3:23)

One of the hardest things about sharing your faith is worrying you'll mess up. What if you share Christ with a friend, but one day you blow it and mess up big-time right in front of her? The truth is that your mistake might be just what she needs to see for a couple of reasons. First, she needs to see that you aren't perfect. There's nothing more annoying or more discouraging than a perfect friend who never messes up. If your friend never sees you fall, she will think she has to be perfect, and feel disappointed already. Second, she needs to see how you react to your sin. Ask forgiveness from her. Show her how you are heartbroken over your sin. Let her see you repent and grow from your mistake. Don't worry about being perfect in front of your friends. Your occasional mistake can teach them as much as your great example.

DAY 109

Drama Queen Bee

[Be] ready at any time to give a defense to anyone who asks you
for a reason for the hope that is in you. (1 Peter 3:15)

She cries all morning in the girls' bathroom at school. She screams and throws things when she doesn't get her way. She reigns high on her emotional throne because she is the drama queen. Have you ever been friends with a drama queen? There's never a dull moment. If she's not crying when you get to school, she'll be crying before the day is over. The next time you have a drama queen moment with your friend, take the opportunity to share Christ with her. Maybe she needs to hear your story of salvation. Give her a Bible verse. A girl is usually ready to listen when she's feeling down. It's usually the perfect opportunity to share words of hope. She may need to hear the hope of a Savior who will be her constant during the ups and downs of a girl's life.

DAY 110

Share Your Life

We cared so much for you that we were pleased to share with you not only the gospel of God but also our own lives, because you had become dear to us. (1 Thessalonians 2:8)

A great way to share your faith is to share your life with a girl who doesn't know Christ. When you hang around girls who don't know Christ, they can see the difference God has made in your life. When she sees your kind spirit, your thankful heart, your patience, and your joy, she will wonder what you have that she doesn't have. She will see how you respond to stressful situations and how you treat your siblings. Be careful that you're the one influencing her, though, and not the other way around. You should still have strong Christian friends as well. Sometimes the gospel isn't about using big words, but it's about showing your life to nonbelievers. Then you can share Christ when the right time comes.

DAY 111

Send Me

Then I heard the voice of the Lord asking: Who should I send? Who will go for us? I said: Here I am. Send me. (Isaiah 6:8)

God is looking for girls who will live for Him. He searches for girls who aren't weighed down by the world's love of money and external beauty. Most girls will follow the crowd and do things their own way. But some girls will follow Christ. They will seek to be near God and to love the things God loves. They will make their lives look like Jesus. They will honor God with their words and their actions. These girls will shine like lights in a dark world. They will take the gospel to their schools, ball fields, and neighborhoods. Can God send you? Will you go for Him to share His love with others? You don't have to be perfect. You just need a heart for Christ. He will do the rest.

Big Decisions

Every day a girl makes hundreds of tiny choices, but sometimes she's faced with a big decision that will impact her life in a major way. This section deals with how to make those tough decisions.

DAY 112

Ask the Right People

Without guidance, a people will fall, but with many counselors there is deliverance. (Proverbs 11:14)

Every day you make hundreds of decisions that impact the course of your day. Every now and then, you're faced with a really big decision. When that time comes, one of the smartest things you can do is seek godly counsel. Rather than rushing into a decision or doing what feels right to you, seek the advice of those who walk with God. What do your parents think? What about your student pastor or children's minister? Listen to the advice of your spiritual mentors and then act on it. Scripture says that without guidance, people fall. Who are the godly people God has placed in your life? The next time you need help with a decision, seek their counsel, and follow their advice.

DAY 113

Seek God's Word

Your word is a lamp for my feet and
a light on my path. (Psalm 119:105)

Have you ever been alone in a room when the power goes out? The first thing you do is freeze. When you can't see, it's not safe to run around in a pitch-black room. God's Word is exactly like a light to us. In a dark and confusing world, when so many people are shouting which way to go, God's Word gives us direction. It tells us how to treat people, how to think, act, and live. It tells us how to be close to God. You can go to God's Word any time about any issue. And the more you read it, the easier it is to understand and apply to your life. Make reading the Bible part of your everyday life. It will be a lamp to your feet and a light on your path.

DAY 114

Stuck

*My help comes from the L*ORD*, the Maker*
of heaven and earth. (Psalm 121:2)

Sometimes you're stuck with a tough decision and you have absolutely no idea what to do. You've listened to your friends and your parents, and you've read the Bible. Still, nothing is clear. Continue to seek God in prayer. Sometimes He is slow to make His will known because He is more interested in your heart than your decision. He is fully able to help you with any decision, but mostly He wants you to love Him and know Him. Spend time sitting in God's presence. Worship Him and praise Him. He made heaven and the earth, and you. He knows exactly what you need and when you need it. The best way to know your next step is to draw close to God.

DAY 115

Wise Up

Hold on to what is good. Stay away from every kind of evil.
(1 Thessalonians 5:21–22)

There are some decisions you don't have to think about. You should not drive your mom's car through the neighborhood if you don't have a license. You should tell someone if your brother starts choking. You shouldn't wear high heels on a hiking trip. These decisions are black and white, meaning they're very clear. In Scripture, there are several black-and-white decisions you don't have to think about. It's never okay to murder, steal, or use bad language. Scripture also clearly tells us to always tithe our money, help the poor, and love our enemies. The more you study the Bible, the more you will know these black-and-white issues. You can also be confident that God will never contradict His Word or ask you to do something that is forbidden in His Word. Never. And the more you follow God's Word, the better you can obey it, and the more you can honor Him with your life and draw others to Him.

The Family of God

We never have to live the Christian life alone. God designed us to follow Christ with other believers as part of His church. This section focuses on the beauty of living your life in community. You matter as part of that body, and you have a job to do.

DAY
116

The Measure of Our Hearts

"By this everyone will know that you are my disciples, if you love one another." (John 13:35)

We use measurements every day to make sure things are working correctly. A gas gauge makes sure you have enough gas in your car. Your report card measures how much you're learning. Your doctor measures your height and weight to make sure you're healthy. God also gives us a measurement for our walk with Him, something that lets us know if we're following Him like we should be. The Bible says we will be known as followers of Christ when we love each other. The more we love other people, the more we love God. The two always go together. To measure your heart for God, the Bible says you can look at how much you love other people. The world also notices. You can't fake love for others. It's only found when you know God. If you want to know how you're doing in your walk with God, simply measure your love for other people. Draw close to God and you will love people more.

DAY 117

No More Comparing

Let each person examine his own work,
and then he can take pride in himself alone,
and not compare himself with someone else. (Galatians 6:4)

Girls are good at ranking each other. In our group of friends, we know who's the prettiest, the funniest, the smartest, and who has the cutest clothes. God doesn't work like this. He only has eyes for you. The Bible says that each person should examine her own work, not in comparison to someone else. Your heart for God and your good actions stand alone. God never says, "Well, you did a good job, but your best friend really did a lot for Me this week." Nor does He say, "You messed up a lot, but at least you weren't as bad as that girl." Nope. God loves you individually. He never compares you to your friends, your siblings, or your parents. Comparing yourself to other girls is dangerous because it can produce arrogance or false guilt. Keep your eyes on Christ and let Him, not other girls, convict and encourage you. Then you can walk with God in the full confidence of who you are in Him.

DAY 118

The Purpose of Our Gifts

So also you—since you are zealous for spiritual gifts,
seek to excel in building up the church. (1 Corinthians 14:12)

If you're a Christian, you have a spiritual gift God gave you when you came to Christ. Paul teaches that God didn't give us these gifts so we would get praise. Our gifts are meant to serve the church. When you're good at something, you're supposed to use it to benefit other Christians, not just yourself. The better you are at something, the better the body of Christ should be. What are you good at? What personality trait or talents do you have? Use those to encourage and serve your Christian friends, your family, and the church. You can tell the greatness of a gift by how much it builds up others in Christ. Instead of ranking each other so you can feel important, serve each other so everyone can be better.

DAY 119

Avoid Stupid Arguments

Reject foolish and ignorant disputes, because you know that they breed quarrels. (2 Timothy 2:23)

Have you ever gotten in a stupid argument? It usually happens when we're tired or hungry and everything gets on our nerves. The Bible tells us to have nothing to do with stupid arguments. He's not really talking about getting irritated with your siblings, although we should avoid that too. He's talking about the silly fights Christians get in over stupid things. When Christians fight, it makes God look bad. The world sees Christians arguing and it thinks they are fake. In the family of God, we're supposed to have unity and to have peace with each other. You may disagree with a brother or sister in Christ, but that doesn't mean you have to fight. Some things just aren't worth getting upset. Make every effort to keep peace with your fellow believers in Christ.

A Girl's Best Friends

Nothing has more power in a girl's life than her friends. This section focuses on the power of choosing wise friends and building each other up to be closer to God.

DAY 120

You Are Whom You Sit Beside

The one who walks with the wise will become wise,
but a companion of fools will suffer harm. (Proverbs 13:20)

If your best friend suddenly decided to knock you down, could she do it? What about ten friends? You'd be pushed over in a second. In the same way, if those friends tried to pick you up, they could easily do it.

Friends are powerful in your life. No matter how strong you might be, a group of friends can always influence you in another direction. That's why it's so important that you choose your friends carefully. Surround yourself with girls who love the Lord. Seek friends who are encouraging, friends who will make you better. If you want to be wise, pure, and godly, choose friends who seek those things too. Your choice of friends now can impact you for many years to come. Friends are also a great way to evaluate yourself. Want to know how you're acting? Take a close look at your friends because chances are, you're just like them. Honor God with your friendships, and choose girls who will push you to know God more.

DAY 121

I Can, but I Won't

*But be careful that this right of yours in no way becomes
a stumbling block to the weak. (1 Corinthians 8:9)*

Now that you're getting older, you're probably allowed to watch more mature shows on TV, not just cartoons with Spanish explorers or puppet shows with green frogs and a giant yellow bird. But when your little brother or sister is around, you still watch the baby shows for their sake. That's because something that seems silly to you might scare them. That's how it is in the Christian life. We might be allowed to do something, but sometimes we choose not to because it makes someone else struggle. If your friend struggles with spending money, you might not want to spend the day shopping—even if shopping isn't really a bad thing. If another friend struggles with an eating disorder, it's not a good idea to go on a diet together. It's not about what you're allowed to do; it's what is helpful to those around you. You never want to make someone else stumble, even if it's not something you struggle with. Think about the choices you make today, and look for ways to encourage your friends to stay close to God.

DAY 122

I Like to Be Around You

For I have great joy and encouragement from your love, because the hearts of the saints have been refreshed through you, brother.
(Philemon 7)

An encouraging friend is refreshing to the spirit. She makes you feel good just by being around her. She sees the positive side of things and almost always has a good attitude, even when things are hard. You just love being around her. You can be this kind of girl in Christ. God wants to encourage others through you. He wants your words and your servant's heart to bring joy to other Christians and to your family. He wants to fill you with joy that's contagious to those around you. If you struggle being positive or you always seem to be in a bad mood, spend time with God. In His presence, you can't help but be cheerful and spread that joy to everyone around you.

DAY 123

How to Rescue a Friend on Fire

Brothers and sisters, if someone is overtaken in any wrongdoing, you who are spiritual, restore such a person with a gentle spirit, watching out for yourselves so that you also won't be tempted. (Galatians 6:1)

Have you ever seen a friend's hair catch on fire when she didn't realize it? While watching it burn, did you text another friend about it? Did you sit there and yell at her for being so stupid for catching on fire? Did you quietly go back to eating and hope she'd eventually notice? No way! You rushed over to her and threw water on her so fast she didn't know what hit her. You didn't want the fire to spread or your friend to get burned.

When you see a friend stumble in her walk with Christ, you want to restore her. The Bible says to gently help her back to Christ. You don't yell at her, talk about her behind her back, or ignore her. Gently confront her and tell her she's doing something dangerous. Tell her you want to help, pray with her, and keep her accountable. But be careful because fire spreads. The Bible says to watch out so that you don't start to struggle with the same thing your friend struggles with. Gently walk beside her and help her overcome her struggle, taking care not to commit the same sins.

DAY 124

The Best Way to Poison Your Friendship

For where there is envy and selfish ambition exist,
there is disorder and every evil practice. (James 3:16)

Jealousy is the poison of friendships. Jealousy is when those same qualities that made you first love your friend—her personality and common interests—suddenly become things you wish you had. Jealousy is wanting to look, act, or be like your friend so much that you can't enjoy the friendship. It's a sin, and it kills your relationship. If you're feeling jealous of a friend, take that feeling to God. One of the quickest ways to kill jealousy is to get on your knees and pray for your friend. It's hard to be jealous of a friend when you pray for her. Another way to tackle jealousy is to stay close to God yourself. The closer you get to God, the more satisfied you are with your personality, talents, intelligence, and the way you look. You can recognize your blessings and be content. You don't need the qualities of your friend. Guard against jealousy, and your friendships will honor God.

DAY 125

You're Really Getting on My Nerves

Therefore, I want the men in every place to pray,
lifting up holy hands without anger or argument. (1 Timothy 2:8)

A girl who never fights with her friends is a girl whose only friends are dolls. Every girl sometimes fights with her friends. The important thing is how we deal with those fights. Do you yell and scream at each other? Do you send angry text messages or spread gossip? Part of being a godly friend means dealing with conflict. Instead of flying off the handle, give your friend some space, then come back to talk about the problem. Listen to her feelings and share yours. Forgive her. When you hold on to a problem, it grows and ruins the whole friendship. It even impacts your relationship with God. Learning to deal with friendship conflict now will serve you the rest of your life. Don't end the friendship over something small. Pray about it, deal with it, and continue to have healthy friendships.

DAY 126

It's All About Her

*Everyone should look out not only for his own interests,
but also for the interests of others. (Philippians 2:4)*

Have you ever known a friend who is all about herself? She constantly talks about herself and wants you to talk about her too. She's absorbed in her own problems. She's selfish and doesn't even realize it. Although this friend is really annoying, the truth is we've all been just like this before. We've all been selfish, soaking up all the attention. The Bible says we're supposed to look to the interests of others. In Christ, we can focus the conversation on other people. You look out for your friends and help them with their problems, even if it means less time talking about you. Have you been an attention-hog with your friends lately? Let God help you put the focus on serving your friends. When you serve them by listening and being there for them, you also show them the love of Christ. That's true friendship.

DAY 127

Let the Competition Begin!

Love one another deeply as brothers and sisters.
Outdo one another in showing honor. (Romans 12:10)

Boys are supposed to be the competitive ones, but girls are absolutely competitive with each other. When your friend makes a 95 on a test and you make a 99, you know you feel good. We compete with our clothes, our shoes, our grades, and our talents. The Bible describes only one kind of healthy competition between friends—a contest of serving. The Bible says we are to outdo each other in showing honor. We're supposed to out-serve each other. When your friend does something nice for you, you do two nice things for her. You forgive her when she makes you mad. You overlook her annoying habits. When she lets you borrow something, you return it in better condition than you got it. This kind of competition makes the world take notice because that's not how friends usually behave—especially girls. No drama, just serving. That's the power of Christ in a friendship. Let the serving game begin!

DAY 128

If It's Online, It Doesn't Count, Right?

*"Just as you want others to do for you,
do the same for them." (Luke 6:31)*

It's tempting to say things online or in a text message that we would never say out loud. Just because we can't see someone face-to-face doesn't mean we can be careless or mean with our words. If your parents let you text message your friends or e-mail, be careful what you say. Be encouraging and respectful with your words. Just because it isn't spoken with your voice doesn't mean it's not your words. What you say, or type, matters, so use your words to build others up in Christ. Never send a message in anger or frustration. If you're not allowed to text or e-mail yet, you will be eventually. Decide in advance to use care when sending messages to others. You reflect the character of Christ in everything you say out loud or on the screen.

DAY 129

A Girl's BFF

Oil and incense bring joy to the heart, and the sweetness of a friend is better than self-counsel. (Proverbs 27:9)

She doesn't care what you wear or if you're having a bad hair day. She shares her lunch with you and laughs at your stupid jokes. She's got your back through good and bad, and you can depend on her. She's your best friend, your BFF, your bestie. Whatever you call her, your best friend loves you for who you are. You have fun together. A true best friend also encourages you in the Lord. She prays for you and gives you godly advice. If you have this kind of best friend, thank God for her. Focus on being a great best friend to her. Friends are meant to encourage us in the Lord and push us to keep on living for Christ. Two are better than one when it comes to following God. So be extra sweet to your best friend today, and thank God for her.

DAY 130

Seriously, I Need a Friend

Turn to me and be gracious to me,
for I am alone and afflicted. (Psalm 25:16)

We've all experienced times when we could use a friend. Maybe you just moved or switched schools. It's tough when you haven't found that close group of girls you can count on. When you're feeling lonely, trust the Lord. Focus on being the kind of friend you want to have. Be kind and let your joy in the Lord shine through. Any girl would be lucky to be your friend. Ask God to give you a strong Christian friend. Look around because it's likely another girl in your class is praying the same thing. Loneliness is painful, but in Christ, you are never alone. He will never leave your side while you wait for your other friends to come along.

DAY 131

We're Going to Take This One to God

For this reason also, since the day we heard this, we haven't stopped praying for you. We are asking that you may be filled with the knowledge of his will in all wisdom and spiritual understanding. (Colossians 1:9)

Sometimes the best thing you can do for your friends is to pray for them. When you have a friend who goes through something hard, get on your knees and pray for her. God hears your prayers for your friend. It's also hard to stay mad at someone you pray for. When you feel angry at your friends, pray over them. Ask God to bring peace to the situation. Good friends can also pray together. It doesn't matter if it's something small like a test or something big like a problem at home, you can come to God with anything. Practice praying for your friends and praying with them. You'll be amazed how strong a friendship grows when you pray together.

DAY 132

You Think I Should Do What?

And I pray this: that your love will keep on growing in knowledge and every kind of discernment, so that you may approve the things that are superior and may be pure and blameless in the day of Christ. (Philippians 1:9–10)

Be careful taking advice from your friends. Sometimes friends mean well, but they don't necessarily give you advice from God's Word. Take all advice before the Word of God before you follow it. See if your friend's advice lines up with what God teaches. Talk to your parents and other strong Christians. If your friend walks with God, you can trust her advice, but you still need to seek God for yourself. No one has the power to influence you like your friends. That's why it's important you know God for yourself so you don't follow anyone blindly, even your best friends. Listen to your friends, but see for yourself if their advice agrees with the Bible.

DAY 133

Please Unfriend Immediately

Do not be deceived: "Bad company corrupts good morals."
(1 Corinthians 15:33)

Some girls are just bad news. They bring you down and make you feel bad about yourself. They don't build you up or encourage you to be close to God. Some friendships just need to end. If you have a toxic friend, or one who is always causing you pain, you need some space. Tell her you need a break from the friendship, no calling, no texting, no hanging out. You are called to be kind to everyone, but you don't have to be everyone's best friend. You are not obligated to be friends with a girl who causes you physical or emotional harm. Pray for her and trust God to heal her, but distance yourself from her. The best thing you can do is to let her go.

DAY 134

When God LOLs

Our mouths were filled with laughter then, and our tongues with shouts of joy. Then they said among the nations, "The LORD has done great things for them." (Psalm 126:2)

Think about the last time you and your best friend laughed the hardest. There is nothing better than stomach-hurting, tears-pouring, funny-snorts kind of laughter. Did you know that God loves laughter? He loves it when we have fun with our friends and laugh together. Following Christ doesn't mean we have to be serious all the time with a frown. It's the opposite. God wants to fill our lives with laughter and joy deeper than anything the world offers. Laughter between friends isn't just fun; it's powerful. It lifts your spirits and pushes gloomy thoughts away. An inside joke can quickly turn a bad day into a hilarious day. So as long as it honors God, laugh it up with your friends. Be silly at the right times, and enjoy the friendships God gave you. He's probably laughing right beside you.

Absolutely Beautiful

Every girl wants to be beautiful. It's vital that we understand true, lasting beauty and run away from cheap, imitation beauty that doesn't last. This section focuses on real, unshakable beauty and how a girl can find it in Christ.

DAY
135

Beauty Without Disguise

Charm is deceptive and beauty is fleeting, but a woman who fears the LORD will be praised. (Proverbs 31:30)

We live in a world that values girls by their external beauty: their size, their hair, their fashion. But there's a kind of beauty that goes deeper than our wardrobe, deeper than our haircut, and deeper than our skin. True beauty is found in Christ. A girl who seeks God will be beautiful by the only opinion that matters—God's. This kind of beauty doesn't depend on the newest styles or the most makeup. The kind of beauty the world seeks is cheap and hollow—it doesn't satisfy, and it doesn't bring joy. But the girl who stays close to God can't help being beautiful because she reflects her Father. What kind of beauty are you seeking?

DAY 136

Pretty for Nothing

"And you, devastated one, what are you doing that you dress yourself in scarlet, that you adorn yourself with gold jewelry, that you enhance your eyes with makeup? You beautify yourself for nothing."
(Jeremiah 4:30)

The cutest clothes, glittery jewelry, and a bag full of makeup can't hide an ugly heart. The Bible says these girls "beautify [themselves] for nothing." We've all known a girl who tried to hide her meanness by being fashionable. It doesn't work, and sooner or later everyone sees through the fake—especially God. Instead of craving physical beauty like the world, focus on becoming beautiful to God. Let Him make you into a young woman of character, joy, honesty, and happiness. He wants to fill you with His confidence, which doesn't come from being the perfect size or having the perfect skin. His love in you is flawless, and He will work to make you flawless. While there's nothing wrong with wanting to dress cute or wear trendy things, make sure you're also making yourself spiritually beautiful. It's the only kind of beauty that really counts, and the only one that lasts.

DAY 137

Beautiful Is Forever

Therefore we do not give up. Even though our outer person is being destroyed, our inner person is being renewed day by day.
(2 Corinthians 4:16)

Have you been around an older lady at your church or in your family who is beautiful? She's probably got gray hair and a few wrinkles. She's probably not wearing skinny jeans or pink leggings. Her beauty doesn't come from being fashionable, super skinny, or glamorous. Her beauty shines from the inside out. She has a joy that's contagious, a personality that people just want to be around. She probably serves others and makes everyone in her presence feel warm. That's the kind of beauty we need to seek. It's the kind of beauty that's only possible in Christ. Although it's hard to imagine, your youth will fade. One day you will have wrinkles. When you spend your life getting closer to Christ, you will have an inner beauty that only grows the older you get. You can have that beauty now. Draw near to God and let Him make you truly beautiful with the light of His presence.

DAY 138

Made Beautiful

Those who look to him are radiant with joy;
their faces will never be ashamed. (Psalm 34:5)

Have you ever stood close to a campfire in the winter, roasting a marshmallow or just getting warm? What happens when you look away? Your face gets cold. When you look closely at a fire, you can't help but get warm. Your face gets that "fire glow" and feels suddenly cold when you turn away to the night air. It's the same in your walk with God. When you spend time in His presence in worship and reading the Word, you are spiritually radiant. You reflect the qualities of God: peace, patience, gentleness, joy. The closer you get to God, the more you look like Him. Scripture says you are "radiant with joy." Feeling a little cold? Maybe you need to spend some time with God today. Play a worship song, or write a prayer in your journal. Soak in His presence, and you will have a radiant "fire glow" the coldness of the world cannot take away.

DAY 139

Beauty Is Modest

The women are to dress themselves in modest clothing,
with decency and good sense, not with elaborate hairstyles,
gold, pearls, or expensive apparel. (1 Timothy 2:9)

Modesty is covering your body so you honor God and protect guys from temptation. It's not wearing shorts or skirts that are too short. It's not wearing anything too tight, see-through, or strapless without an under-shirt or a cover. Modesty is refusing to flaunt your body for attention. Right now, you may have no desire whatsoever to attract attention to your body; you may even want to hide it! It's important to learn about modesty now, so you can practice good habits all the time. In order to be modest with your outfits, many times you just have to listen to your parents. At this point in your life, they understand more than you do about what is mod-est. Trust them when they say you can't wear something. They protect your purity and your heart. Modesty is beauty.

DAY 140

Beauty Is Humble

Let another praise you, and not your own mouth—a stranger, and not your own lips. (Proverbs 27:2)

We live in a world where it's cool to brag about yourself. Whether it's hundreds of selfies on Instagram, bragging on Twitter, or just talking about yourself in person, everyone seems to be screaming about their own accomplishments. But there's a quiet, yet striking beauty in humility. Humility means you don't put yourself first and you don't call attention to your own good deeds. You let your actions speak for themselves and wait for others to praise you. What would your day be like if you pointed out the beauty in your friends instead of waiting for them to praise you? What if you stood back and let someone else speak first? Humility is a beautiful and rare quality, only possible inside a relationship with God. Ask Him to give you the beauty of humility and watch Him transform you to put others first.

DAY 141

A Beautiful Mind

*Set your minds on things above, not on earthly things.
(Colossians 3:2)*

*The mind-set of the flesh is death, but the mind-set
of the Spirit is life and peace. (Romans 8:6)*

If you've ever played a sport, you've probably heard your coach say something like, "Think like a winner!" Before you step onto the field or court, you have to think winning thoughts. That means you have a strategy about how to play and you mentally prepare to face your opponent. The same is true in our walk with God. Our minds are the starting point for everything we face in the day. If we fill our minds with the things of God—Scripture, praise, worship, thanksgiving, and prayer—then we will live and act those things out in our lives. We will forgive easily, show patience, have joy, honor our parents, etc. If we fill our minds with gossip, negative thoughts, and the world's idols, we will live that out in our lives as well. Choose to fill your mind with holy things. Concentrate on who God is and what His Word says. Then you will see those thoughts become reality in your life, and the enemy will be no match for you.

DAY 142

A Beautiful Heart

"I will give you a new heart and put a new spirit within you;
I will remove your heart of stone and give you a heart of flesh."
(Ezekiel 36:26)

As for you, LORD, you know me; you see me.
You test whether my heart is with you. (Jeremiah 12:3)

When someone asks, "Is she pretty?" and the response is, "Awww, she has a good heart," we all know what that means, and it's not good. But seriously, having a beautiful heart doesn't mean you're not beautiful on the outside too. A beautiful heart is a heart that's been captured by God. It means you love the things God loves. You delight in Him, and it shows in your life. The start of true beauty happens in your heart. It's the essence of who you are. When you have a heart for God, you have a heart for other people. The only way to have a beautiful heart is through Christ. He takes your old heart and gives you a new one. He loves you so much, He wants to captivate your heart with Himself. Focus on having a beautiful heart and your life will follow.

DAY 143

Temple of God

Don't you know that your body is a temple of the Holy Spirit
who is in you, whom you have from God? You are not your own.
(1 Corinthians 6:19)

The desire to be thin is strong. For some girls, it's an all-consuming obsession. They think if they can just lose weight and stay skinny, they will feel beautiful. It's a lie and a disease. The desire to be thin can drive girls to exercise excessively and to starve themselves. If this is something you struggle with, you need to talk to a strong Christian mentor and get help. It's not something you have to deal with on your own. If you are in Christ, His Holy Spirit lives inside you. His presence dwells within you, which makes your body the temple of God. He loves you so much that His presence makes you beautiful. He wants to fill you with a confidence and a joy that you can't attain by losing weight. The obsession to be thin starts in your mind. It is a disease that has a cure. Talk to your parents and get godly counsel. And know that God loves you so much, He desires to heal you completely. He wants to help you see the beauty He sees every time He looks at you.

DAY 144

Not Feeling So Beautiful Today

The king will desire your beauty.
Bow down to him, for he is your lord. (Psalm 45:11)

Sometimes a girl just wants to feel pretty—not pretty in her heart, or beautiful in her mind, but really, physically beautiful on the outside. We all want gorgeous hair, flawless skin, and big shiny eyes. We were created to desire real external beauty. If you want to be pretty, that doesn't make you arrogant; it makes you a girl. So what happens when you don't feel beautiful—when your physical body doesn't measure up to the world's standard of beauty. When you look in the mirror, you have to believe God. The world is designed to make you hate your body. If you let movies, magazines, and your friends define your beauty, you will never feel beautiful. God calls you beautiful. He created you, designed you, and made you in His image. He picked the color of your hair, your eyes, your height, and your smile. He did not mess up. Refuse to speak negative words about yourself. Don't step on the world's scale of beauty or let them measure you. Ask God to help you see yourself the way He sees you and to fill you with His confidence. You are His creation—not just on the inside, but on the outside too.

DAY 145

Beautifully Hidden

For you died, and your life is hidden
with Christ in God. (Colossians 3:3)

The world's motto of beauty is "If you've got it, flaunt it." The world tells you to show off your favorite feature like your eyes, hair, legs, or any other part you want to attract attention. In Christ, beauty doesn't work like this. If you want to be beautiful, you hide. The Bible says when you come to God, your life is hidden with Christ. The more you hide your life behind the life of Christ, the more beautiful you are. The more you look like Him, speak like Him, serve like Him, forgive like Him, the more your beauty shines through. True beauty is Christ's beauty. Instead of drawing attention to your own physical beauty, you seek to be covered with the beauty of Christ. That doesn't mean you don't brush your hair or paint your nails or wear cute clothes, but you don't call attention to your body. You don't wear pounds of makeup or immodest clothes because you know that true beauty is deeper than your skin. It's who you are. Hide behind Christ and you will become beautiful.

DAY 146

The Picture Filter

The L<small>ORD</small> said to Samuel, "Do not look at his appearance or his stature because I have rejected him. Human do not see what the L<small>ORD</small> sees, for humans see what is visible, but the L<small>ORD</small> sees the heart." (1 Samuel 16:7)

There's a way to make pictures look amazing called the filter. When you put a filter on a digital picture, you can hide any imperfections, and it gives the whole picture a rosy glow. Filters are great to use, but the truth is that when you use a filter, it's not the real picture. Sometimes we try to put a filter over our lives to make them look better. We put on a smile and act one way on the outside, when inside we feel totally different. Know that God always sees behind every filter. He's never fooled by what's on the outside. He looks at what's in your heart, and that's what matters to Him. Come to Christ and let Him make you beautiful on the inside so you can show His love and do His work on the outside—no filter needed.

Born to Be Free

There's something every girl wants more than cute clothes and a cell phone: FREEDOM. This section talks about the boundaries God gives us that actually make us free.

DAY
147

Born to Be Free

Obey your leaders and submit to them, since they keep watch over your souls as those who will give an account, so that they can do this with joy and not with grief, for that would be unprofitable for you.
(Hebrews 13:17)

Did you know that your parents have to answer to God for how they raise you? God has given them the job of keeping you safe, teaching you about Christ, and showing you what a godly life looks like. That's a pretty exhausting task. Sometimes your parents need you to cut them some slack. They don't always know what they're doing, and sometimes they mess up. You mess up too. They want you to become a beautiful follower of Christ, inside and out. They want you to serve God with your life. They want you to be safe and happy. At any moment, your parents would gladly die for you. They probably love you more than anyone else loves you except for God Himself. Listen to them and obey them. Be patient with them and slow to get angry. Pray for your parents. Encourage them and tell them when they do a good job. Every time you obey them, you honor God too.

DAY 148

Trusted with More

"Whoever is faithful in very little is also faithful in much, and whoever is unrighteous in very little is also unrighteous in much."
(Luke 16:10)

Have you ever let a friend borrow five dollars? If she doesn't pay you back, are you going to let her borrow twenty dollars next week? No way! If you can't be faithful with a little, you can't be trusted with more. This is exactly how it works with your parents. Every time you obey them with something small—making your bed, doing your homework, being kind to your siblings, clearing the table after dinner—you prove that you can be trusted. Each act of obedience shows you are maturing. Your parents recognize that you can be trusted with a little, so they will slowly give you more freedom. Be faithful in the rules they already have for you. If you can't follow small rules with a good attitude, you will never earn more freedom.

Do I Really Still Have to Hold Your Hand?

Children, obey your parents as you would the Lord, because this is right. Honor your father and mother, which is the first commandment with a promise, so that it may go well with you and that you may have a long life in the land. (Ephesians 6:1–3)

Have you ever felt like your parents still treat you like a child? It's frustrating when their rules get in the way of your freedom. The older you get, the more freedom you expect to have. When it comes to rules, God's Word is clear: obeying your parents honors God. Your parents aren't trying to treat you like a child.

Do you want to know the secret to getting more freedom? Listen closely: to get more freedom, joyfully obey the rules you have now. The key word? *Joyfully*. When you roll your eyes, complain, and whine, you show immaturity. When you peacefully follow their rules day after day, you show that you can be trusted. Attitude is everything. Trust your parents, and honor them, and let God give you a good attitude in the process. Before you know it, more freedom will follow.

Don't Tell Me What to Do

*In the same way, you who are younger, be subject to the elders.
All of you clothe yourselves with humility toward one another,
because God resists the proud but gives grace to the humble.*
(1 Peter 5:5)

It's hard to submit to authority. Whether it's a teacher, a parent, a friend's parent, or someone at church, nobody likes somebody else telling them what to do. In Christ, however, submission is a beautiful thing and it honors God. When you obey someone in authority, even if it goes against what you want to do, you are honoring God. The Bible tells us to clothe ourselves with humility. That means we have to get rid of our selfishness and our need to have our own way. Who are the leaders in your life? Honor God by submitting to their instructions with a good attitude. You will reflect Christ and receive the grace of God.

DAY 151

Hot Pink Slavery

Now the Lord is the Spirit, and where the Spirit of the Lord is, there is freedom. (2 Corinthians 3:17)

Girls crave freedom. We want to choose our own clothes, our friends, and where we go. We dislike anyone or anything that threatens to take away that freedom. The truth is that so-called freedom outside of Christ is a lie. Chains can be hot pink or zebra-stripped, but they're still chains. That means that slavery can look like freedom—no rules, wearing what you want, doing whatever you want when you want. It sounds nice, but it's slavery in disguise and it doesn't bring peace. The Bible says where the Spirit of the Lord is, there is freedom. Freedom is only found in Him. Within His rules and His guide for living, we find freedom. Freedom isn't the absence of rules; it's the presence of the right kind of rules that bring true joy and protection. So submit to the freedom in Christ. Obey your parents and the Word of God. When His Spirit lives inside you, you are truly free.

DAY
152

Busted!

*No discipline seems enjoyable at the time, but painful.
Later on, however, it yields the peaceful fruit of righteousness
to those who have been trained by it. (Hebrews 12:11)*

"I love getting in trouble."
"I love it when my parents make rules I don't understand."
"I love it when I want to do something but I'm not allowed to."
—Things No Girl Ever Said

No one likes to get in trouble. It's frustrating, especially when you don't agree with the rule in the first place. Actually, though you might not realize it, discipline is a form of love. If your parents didn't love you, they wouldn't care what you did. They'd let you go ahead and touch that hot stove as many times as you wanted because they wouldn't care how much pain you felt. It's the same with God. He disciplines us because He wants to spare us future unnecessary pain. He knows our lives bring us the most joy when we obey His commands. He will intervene with discipline when we step outside His rules. So instead of flying off the handle the next time you get in trouble, ask God to show you where you stepped away from His commands. Look for the opportunity to grow closer to God so you don't have to feel that same kind of pain again.

Made by Design

You were created by God. Knowing how He made you is the key to knowing your own value in Christ. This section tells you how God made you and the blessings you get as His creation.

DAY 153

In His Image

So God created man in his own image; he created him in the image of God; he created them male and female. (Genesis 1:27)

Have you ever tried to copy the image of a famous person? Maybe you picked a certain haircut from a celebrity photo. Maybe you chose your outfit or jewelry because a particular movie star wore something similar. Maybe you have a friend who's obsessed with a certain star and tries to copy them exactly (annoying, right?). As hard as you try, you can never copy a famous person's exact image. But guess what? There's someone a lot more important whose image you wear every single day. The Bible says you were made in God's image. When He created you, He put His very image into you. Your creativity? Your ability to think? Your personality? Your desire for relationships? All evidence of His image in you. The next time you feel bad about yourself, remember that your Creator put His very image on you. That's how valuable you are. That's how beautiful you are.

DAY 154

With a Purpose

"For I know the plans I have for you"—this is the LORD's declaration—"plans for your well-being, not for disaster, to give you a future and a hope." (Jeremiah 29:11)

You really were created with a purpose. God knows all the days of your life and all the steps you will take. He doesn't just know what will happen in your day; He is in charge of your day. He holds every second, every day, every year of your life in His hands. He has a plan for you and promises hope and a future. Did you know that the verse above from Jeremiah was written at a time when things weren't going so well for God's people? Even when you're having a bad day or a bad week, you can have confidence that God does have a plan for you. Sometimes the greatest blessings come from the toughest times.

DAY 155

Fingerprints of the Creator

My bones were not hidden from you when I was made in secret,
when I was formed in the depths of the earth. (Psalm 139:15)

Way before you were born, God knew you. He saw the color of your hair, your eyes, and your smile. He didn't just see you; He made you. He also formed your personality. He made the sound of your laugh and He loved it. He made you exactly as you are. No accidents. No mistakes. No part of you is unknown to God. The next time you look in the mirror and feel insecure, just think about this: the hands that created the oceans, the planets, the sun, and the stars are the very same hands that formed you. You are wonderfully made, and you carry the fingerprints of the Creator on you.

DAY 156

All That Talent

According to the grace given to us, we have different gifts:
If prophecy, use it according to the proportion of one's faith;
if service, use it in service; if teaching, in teaching; if exhorting,
in exhortation; giving, with generosity; leading, with diligence;
showing mercy, with cheerfulness. (Romans 12:6–8)

Have you ever seen a reality talent show competition? The most popular contestants are almost always the ones who can sing or dance. I'm not sure who decided that these were the most important talents. What if you can't sing or dance? If you have a relationship with God, through Jesus, then you have gifts and talents that have nothing to do with singing and dancing. You have spiritual gifts God has given you to serve other believers. These gifts might be teaching the Bible to friends or children younger than you, encouraging others, showing mercy, praying, serving, or giving. How do you know what gifts you have? Just keep walking with God, stay connected to church, and you will discover your gifts. What if you feel like God forgot you? He didn't. God's Word is clear that every believer has spiritual gifts. Remember that these gifts aren't to make you famous or bring attention to yourself, but they are to serve other believers and draw attention to God. But when you serve using your gifts, you get a lot of joy too.

DAY 157

Never Invisible

"I am the good shepherd. I know my own, and my own know me, just as the Father knows me, and I know the Father. I lay down my life for the sheep." (John 10:14–15)

Have you ever felt like no one notices you? It's easy to feel invisible sometimes, and it hurts. You might feel invisible at school or even in your own family, but you are never invisible to God. The Bible says that Jesus knows His own sheep (that's you). He doesn't just have your name in a grade book—He knows everything about you. And this kind of knowledge isn't just intellectual facts like someone who knows everything about fashion, movies, or their favorite band. Jesus is invested in you. He cares about you inside and outside. He wants to be intimately involved in every detail of your life. You aren't one girl lost in the crowd to Him; you are one in a million. Let this truth sink in. Jesus knows you. And as the Scripture says, He laid down His life for you. You are not invisible anymore.

DAY 158

The Edge of Glory

"[Bring] everyone who bears my name and is created for my glory. I have formed them; indeed, I have made them." (Isaiah 43:7)

You were created to give glory to God. That means you were born to praise Him, born to call attention to God and make Him famous. The world seeks to glorify themselves or make their own names famous. They seek praise and attention for themselves. But God is the only one who deserves glory. How can you give God glory? In everything you do. Every time you show kindness, help someone in need, or speak encouraging words, you give God glory. When you share your faith with friends, when you obey your parents, when you choose to forgive instead of hold a grudge, you are giving God glory. You were created to give glory to God, created to think about Him, speak about Him, worship Him, and make your life about Him.

DAY 159

On the Outside

So then you are no longer foreigners and strangers, but fellow citizens with the saints, and members of God's household.
(Ephesians 2:19)

Have you ever felt left out by your friends? There's no worse feeling. The people who are supposed to be there for you forget to include you. You feel like you're on the outside. Did you know that you were once? Before you came to Christ, you were separate from God by your sin. But when you come to Him, you are always included, now and forever. The Bible says, you're not only included as friends but you are "members of God's household." You're welcomed into His family. The next time you feel left out, remember that God who loves you and saved you will never turn His back on you or forget to include you. You are His daughter, and you always have a place in His family.

DAY 160

Seated with Christ

He also raised us up with him and seated us with him in the heavens in Christ Jesus. (Ephesians 2:6)

Important people sit with other important people. When the president attends a dinner, he's going to sit next to his family or someone on his staff. When famous people attend fancy award ceremonies, they sit next to other famous people. Do you know who the Bible says that Jesus—the Son of God—will sit next to in heaven? You. God's Word says that He has raised us up and seated us with Christ in heaven. That doesn't mean we'll be sitting forever in heaven; it just means that you have been raised to the same status as Christ. In Him, you are forgiven and made clean from your sins so you can be next to Christ. You are important enough that God put you next to His own Son. Never doubt your value in Christ. Through Jesus, you have great worth to your heavenly Father.

DAY 161

Meant to Fly

I am able to do all things through him who strengthens me.
(Philippians 4:13)

An airplane isn't meant to drive up and down a road. Your English book isn't designed to be used as a coaster to hold your soda. Airplanes are meant to fly. English books help you learn English. In the same way, there are things you can't do because you weren't created to do them. Maybe you can't sing or run fast. But you were created to do something else. You were designed to do something that's totally unique to you. When you try to do something you weren't made to do, you'll waste your purpose and feel like a failure. The Bible says you can do all things through Christ. That means that everything God has planned for you to do, you can do. You can endure anything, find joy in anything, and accomplish the plans He has for you. Stop trying to do something you were never meant to do, and discover God's purpose for you. In His strength, you can accomplish it.

Sweet Dreams

Girls dream big dreams, but God's dreams for you are bigger than you could imagine. This section deals with surrendering our dreams for God's and trusting that He holds our future.

DAY 162

Wherever You Go

This God, our God forever and ever—
he will always lead us. (Psalm 48:14)

It's fun to have dreams about where you want to go and who you want to be. God delights to help you dream big dreams for the future. Be confident that He is the one who holds your hand and guides you to the future. He has a plan for your life and a destiny for you. It will include trials and pain as well as beauty and success. The Lord is your anchor through it all. What dreams do you have for your future? Bring them to the Lord. Make plans with God and then trust those plans to God. He will do more than you could ask or imagine in your life.

DAY 163

Seek First

"Seek first the kingdom of God and his righteousness, and all these things will be provided for you." (Matthew 6:33)

As girls who follow Christ, we should have big dreams for ourselves. We need to plan for the future and think about what we want to become someday. The Bible is all about us dreaming of our futures, but it gives one truth that makes those dreams come true: seek first the kingdom of God. When you seek God before everything else, your dreams will come true because they will match God's dreams for your life. Seek Him with your whole heart and never let any lesser love come between you. You are precious to your heavenly Father. He will give you the dreams of your heart, then make them come true.

DAY 164

More Than You Can Imagine

Now to him who is able to do above and beyond all that we ask or think according to the power that works in us. (Ephesians 3:20)

God wants to do more in your life than you ever thought possible. His dreams for you are always greater than your dreams for yourself. That's because His dreams are about making Himself famous, not making you famous. He wants to use your talents, personality, and possessions to spread His message about Christ to the world. What prayers do you need answered? What goals do you have? Commit them to God. He is able to do more than you could possibly ask or imagine according to His power, not ours. Trust Him with every dream and every need. He will not fail to work all things to your good and to the glory of His name.

DAY 165

He Holds Your Future

Commit your activities to the LORD, and your plans will be established.
(Proverbs 16:3)

Every day we think about the future. We study so we'll pass a future test. We get food so we can eat future meals. We make plans with our friends and family. Every day we're also planning for the far-away future, though we might not realize it. Decisions we make every day will impact us in the future. The kind of girl you will be in the future is the girl you're becoming today. Right now you are building the character of the future wife, mom, employee, or church member you will be someday. The great thing about walking with God is that we don't have to worry about the future as we plan. When we commit our lives to Him, He will give us a future that brings Him glory. What kind of future are you making right now? Commit your plans to the Lord.

All That Bling

The lure of money and possessions is strong. No amount of money and no possessions can satisfy like the presence of God. This section helps us recognize the temptation of greed and how to find contentment in Christ alone.

DAY 166

What I Want

Godliness with contentment is great gain. (1 Timothy 6:6)

Have you ever begged your parents for something you really wanted, but when you got it, it was a major disappointment? That's how it works with stuff. It satisfies us for a little while, but that joy always fades and we need something else to bring it back. When you follow Christ and seek Him, you have a satisfaction that never fades. He is able to put true contentment into your heart. No matter what you have or don't have, you can find contentment in Him. The Bible says that godliness with contentment is great gain. When you're living a godly life and you're full of joy, you are richer than any millionaire. In fact, that's what the whole world is desperate for, and you have it. So the next time you're tempted to seek stuff to fill your needs, remember that the key to true joy is found in Christ. You have full access to that joy all day, every day. Now that's real bling.

DAY 167

Your Stuff Is Better

The little that the righteous person has is better than
the abundance of many wicked people. (Psalm 37:16)

It's really hard when one of your parent's gets laid off from work. It's stressful on the whole family. You might have to sell your house, stop buying new clothes, and eat cheaper food. But the Bible says that even when you're poor in the eyes of the world, you are rich in Christ. The few possessions you have are actually better than all the stuff a wicked millionaire owns. Why did God say this? When you have Christ in your life, you have riches the world cannot match. Not only that, but even the physical possessions you have are more valuable because you have God. You see the worth of your stuff and you're thankful. When you're poor in Christ, your possessions don't own you. You trust God and the riches of His blessings, not money, to fulfill you. Without Christ, the rich are slaves to their money. So if you're going through a tough financial time, know that God will bless you when you trust Him.

DAY 168

What She Has

*Those who want to be rich fall into temptation,
a trap, and many foolish and harmful desires, which plunge
people into ruin and destruction. (1 Timothy 6:9)*

A lot of people want to be filthy rich. Turn on the TV and you'll see people doing stupid stuff just to make money. For the world, money promises happiness, satisfaction, and peace. But it's a false promise. The Bible says that people who want to be rich fall into a trap that eventually leads to their ruin and destruction. Riches do not bring peace. Only Christ brings peace the world is so thirsty for. Seek the Lord instead of riches. When you seek Him, a funny thing happens—you discover you're already rich. You've been forgiven, covered by the blood of the Savior. You have access to the God of the universe any time you want to meet with Him. You have unending joy, peace, and love. You have a Father who fights for you, who protects you. Money can't buy any of these things. Avoid the trap that leads to destruction. Seek the riches of a relationship with God, not earthly wealth, and you will be rich indeed.

DAY
169

The Filthy Rich

Do not be afraid when a person gets rich,
when the wealth of his house increases. (Psalm 49:16)

We live in a world obsessed with the rich and famous. Some people are famous for absolutely no reason. We watch reality shows dedicated to people with extravagant lives. We follow what they drive, what they wear, and where they live. It's time for Christians to stop being so awe-stricken by the lives of the wealthy. Every penny in this world belongs to God. He owns it all. True joy, peace, and meaning have nothing to do with a bank account. Are you living like you believe that? Do you attach happiness to having a nicer cell phone, newer clothes, or a huge house? Are you putting pressure on your parents to buy you things so you'll be happy? Riches do not bring satisfaction. Instead of chasing after money and admiring those who do, find your contentment in Christ alone. He is not impressed with wealth when it is used for selfish gain. We shouldn't be either.

Less Is More

*For the love of money is a root of all kinds of evil,
and by craving it, some have wandered away from the faith and
pierced themselves with many griefs. (1 Timothy 6:10)*

No one has ever been attacked by a wad of dollar bills. That's because money itself isn't bad. It's not out to get you or destroy your life, but it can when you love it. The Bible says the love of money is evil, in fact its the root of all evil. You love money when you want to be rich. You love money when you're not happy with what you already have and want newer, nicer stuff. You love money when you don't help someone in need because you want to keep more for yourself. Having money isn't bad, but loving money is. The Bible teaches that where your treasure is, there your heart will be. If you treasure money, it will capture your heart as well. The best way to fight against the love of money? Give stuff away. When you have a thankful heart and give generously to people in need, you will never fall in love with money. When you stay close to God, He becomes your treasure and money will never have your heart.

DAY
171

God Meets Your Needs

And my God will supply all your needs according to His riches in glory in Christ Jesus. (Philippians 4:19)

God knows what we need before we ask Him. He knows our physical needs: food, clothes, a safe home. He also knows our social need for friends. He knows our emotional needs for peace, joy, and love. He knows our spiritual needs for intimacy with God, forgiveness for our sins, and our need to worship. He delights to meet our needs. In fact, He's the only one who can. Sometimes we confuse needs with wants. Like a child sometimes wants to touch a hot oven, sometimes we want things that will cause us harm. God hates to make us sad, but He will not let us have something that will hurt us. Do you have a need that God isn't meeting right now? Pray to Him and tell Him how you feel. More than anything, our biggest need isn't a person, a feeling, or more stuff—it's God Himself. He will never withhold His love or His presence from us. He will always meet our needs according to His plan and His riches.

DAY 172

God's Bank Account

"The silver and gold belong to me"—this is the declaration of the Lord of Armies. (Haggai 2:8)

Who is the richest person you know? A movie star? A musician? A king or queen? Someone who invented something important? Your God is richer than all of them put together. He owns all the gold, all the diamonds, and all the cash. His bank account is always full. Girl, your daddy is loaded. He can give to anyone He wants and He can take away. The next time you're stressed about money, remember that your Father owns it all. He loves you so much. He knows that what you really need isn't material wealth, but spiritual wealth. Trust Him to provide for your needs. When He blesses you, be generous with other people. It all belongs to Him anyway.

DAY 173

Bring the Tithe

"Bring the full tenth into the storehouse so that there may be food in my house. Test me in this way," says the LORD of Armies. "See if I will not open the floodgates of heaven and pour out a blessing for you without measure." (Malachi 3:10)

It's not often God says, "Test me." When He does, we need to pay attention. In this verse, God challenges His people to test Him with their money by tithing. Tithing is giving 10 percent of the money you earn to the "storehouse" or to the church. It's not because God needs your money—He already owns it all. When you give 10 percent of your money back to the church, you're telling God that He is in control of your money. You honor Him and prove that money is not your god. Then God says He will pour out blessings on you. These blessings might not be more money. Often the blessings of tithing are spiritual and freedom from slavery to your money. Maybe you're thinking, *I don't have any money. I'm broke.* Actually, the best time to learn about tithing is before you have any money. Then you will know God's will when you get your first job. When you do earn a little money by babysitting or doing chores, you can practice tithing. When you learn the joy of tithing now, you can experience the blessings the rest of your life.

DAY 174

Made Rich So You Can Give

You will be enriched in every way for all generosity, which produces thanksgiving to God through us. (2 Corinthians 9:11)

Have you ever seen a child give their cookie to another kid who doesn't have one? The parents usually rush in, praise the child for sharing, and give him a whole handful of cookies. That's what God does for us. He sees when we share our stuff with people in need. He knows when we let our sister or brother have something we really wanted. How does He respond to our giving? He just wants to give us more! Sometimes when we give, God gives us more stuff, but sometimes He gives us a lot of joy, peace, and friendship. Sometimes God gives us something just to watch us give it away. He knows that we're more blessed when we give than when we keep it for ourselves. What can you give to someone in need today? You will be blessed.

DAY 175

Dollar-Sign Diva

Turn my heart to your decrees and
not to dishonest profit. (Psalm 119:36)

We live in a world starving for more: more technology, more stuff, and most of all more money. As girls, we can get caught up in the "more" disease. It's easy to get swept away with all the stuff we want—clothes, the latest phone, shoes, anything our friends have that we don't. We start to overlook what we do have, and we're ungrateful to our parents. That's why God tells us in the Bible to turn our hearts to His Words. He alone is able to cure our "more" disease. He satisfies us and keeps us from continually craving everything the worlds sets before us. The world praises a material girl, a girl who seeks everything she wants. But the truth is that a material, me-focused girl is pretty ugly to be around. Focus your attention on the truth of God. Let Him turn your "more" attitude into a thankful attitude.

My Style

We pay attention to what we wear. Even if we throw on a T-shirt and sweat pants, we do it on purpose. Clothes say a lot about who we are. This section addresses the clothes and accessories we wear in Christ, physically and spiritually, so we can reflect Him to a lost world.

DAY 176

Fashion Scents

For to God we are the fragrance of Christ among those who are being saved and among those who are perishing. (2 Corinthians 2:15)

What is the sweetest smell you can imagine? Whether it's chocolate chip cookies baking in the oven, new lotion or shampoo in your favorite scent, or a Christmas candle filling the house with yummy fragrance, good smells just put us in a better mood. Did you know that when you come to Christ and walk with God, you wear a spiritual scent that is sweeter than any smell on the earth? The Bible says that you are the "fragrance of Christ" to the lost world. That doesn't mean you can stop wearing deodorant or taking showers. But it does mean that you are radically different from those around you who don't know God. When you have His peace, His love, His joy, and His patience in your life, you are beautiful to the world. Like a sweet smell in a junk yard, you are refreshing and you have something the world desperately needs. Today, have confidence that you are a sweet smell to your friends, teachers, and neighbors who don't know God. Then dare to love them and tell them the good news of Christ.

DAY 177

A Holy Pedicure

How beautiful on the mountains are the feet of the herald, who proclaims peace, who brings news of good things, who proclaims salvation, who says to Zion, "Your God reigns!" (Isaiah 52:7)

Most of the time feet are disgusting. They are stuffed inside our shoes all day. They walk on the nasty ground. They usually don't smell very nice (especially boy feet). But once in awhile, feet can actually be pretty. If you've ever had a pedicure, you know how relaxing it is. Someone professionally washes, massages, and pampers your feet. Then they paint your toes any color you want. You walk away thinking, *My feet look hot.* It's a great feeling having pretty feet.

Did you know God thinks certain feet are beautiful? It has nothing to do with the way they smell or if they're freshly painted. The feet God finds beautiful belong to the girl who shares Christ. In other words, when you walk around all day living for God and sharing the love of Christ, you have beautiful feet! So as you go throughout your day, speaking kind words, encouraging friends, showing patience, and most of all sharing Christ, know that even your feet are beautiful to God.

DAY 178

Covered Girl

The women are to dress themselves in modest clothing, with decency and good sense, not with elaborate hairstyles, gold, pearls, or expensive apparel, but with good works, as is proper for women who profess to worship God. (1 Timothy 2:9–10)

Pick up any secular teen magazine and you will see that today's girls don't care about modesty. For Christians, modesty means dressing in a way that covers your body and doesn't tempt guys sexually. The world encourages young girls to dress sexy and show skin. This is the opposite of what God's Word teaches. Learning how to dress modestly usually means listening to your parents. Sometimes you might choose an outfit that is totally harmless to you, but your parents ask you to change anyway. Trust them. Even though your intentions are pure, they can understand more than you about modesty at this point. When you honor God with your clothes, it's great to be stylish and cute as well. You don't have to wear a paper bag. Learn to dress modestly, trust your parents, and you will be a light for Christ in a dark world.

DAY 179

Covered with Christ

Put on the Lord Jesus Christ, and don't make plans
to gratify the desires of the flesh. (Romans 13:14)

The Bible tells us to put on the Lord Jesus Christ. That doesn't mean like a coat or a sweater. It means that every day you intentionally cover your life with His life. You exchange your desires, your selfishness, and your dreams for His desires, His plans, and His dreams. You cover your sin with His holiness. You remember that He went to the cross for you, to pay for your sins so you could have perfect intimacy with God. When you put on the Lord Jesus, you are clothed with peace, joy, and patience. He makes you beautiful from the inside out. He fills you with kind words and a gentle spirit. Have you covered yourself with Christ today? It's pretty easy to tell. Do you think, act, and speak like Him? When you put on Christ, you are a new creation, and you make the people around you want to know Him more.

DAY 180

Over the Shoulder

Cast your burden on the LORD, and he will sustain you;
he will never allow the righteous to be shaken. (Psalm 55:22)

As girls, we carry a lot of things every day. On a school day, you probably carry a backpack loaded down with heavy books, notebooks, pencils, journals, your lunch. You might carry a purse—a girl's best friend—filled with a wallet, makeup, gum, and keys. Every day our arms are full with the things we carry. But what about the things we carry that no one can see, things like anger, frustration, and stress. Is there something or someone who is upsetting you? Jealousy, fear, and anxiety can weigh us down. Just because we don't carry them in our arms doesn't mean they're not heavy. The Bible says we don't have to carry these things any more. In Christ, God is able to take the hidden things that weigh us down, the burdens that we carry on our hearts. He can lift them off our shoulders. When you get home from school and drop your heavy backpack on the ground, you immediately feel light again. God can do the same thing to your heart when you trust Him. Give your worries to Him. He will take them from you.

Home Sweet Home

Our families know us better than anyone else in the world. Sometimes that's a blessing, and sometimes it's just annoying. This section deals with the joys and frustrations of our families.

DAY 181

Famous Parents

I recall your sincere faith that first lived in your grandmother Lois and in your mother Eunice and now, I am convinced, is in you also. (2 Timothy 1:5)

It can be hard when our parents are famous. I'm not talking about in movies or sports, but famous at church and in the community. When everyone knows your parents, it can be easy for people to assume things about you too. Maybe you've heard, "Oh, you're so-and-so's daughter, so you shouldn't be doing that." It's pretty annoying. Timothy in the Bible understood. He was a third-generation Christian, meaning his mother and grandmother were well-known for their faith in the community. But Timothy couldn't just rely on their faith; he had to find Christ for himself.

Just because your parents are "famous" at church doesn't mean their faith applies to you. You have to know God for yourself. Your journey with God won't be an exact copy of your parents either. God cares about you because you're you—not because your parents go to church. Thank God for your parents' faith, but follow God for yourself and experience all He has for you.

DAY 182

How You Can Bless Your Home

No one is to seek his own good,
but the good of the other person. (1 Corinthians 10:24)

"Make your bed," "Vacuum the floor," "Clear the table"—words no girl wants to hear. Sometimes it's easier to serve a complete stranger than it is to serve our own families. But serving starts at home. You have the power to help make your home a warm, kind place. When you serve your family, you are being the hands and feet of Christ. How would your mom react if you set the table without being asked? What if you folded your brother's laundry? Sometimes a small act of kindness can change the attitude of the whole house. It might be possible to put on a godly act at school or in church, but it's really hard to fake being nice at home. When you genuinely follow God, it will show in how you treat your family and how you serve around the house. Don't miss out on the joy of serving your family. They will see the difference Christ has made in you.

DAY 183

Did My Parents Really Do That in Public?

Now we ask you, brothers and sisters, to give recognition to those
who labor among you and lead you in the Lord and admonish you.
(1 Thessalonians 5:12)

Sometimes your parents are just plain annoying. Maybe you feel like they're not listening or maybe they way overreacted to something that wasn't a big deal. Maybe they totally embarrassed you in front of your friends (the worst). Even when they get on your nerves, your parents are still placed in your life by God. They are in authority over you and are meant to teach you the instruction of the Lord. Even when you wish they weren't, they're still your parents. The Bible teaches that we are to honor them and give recognition or respect to those who are over us in the Lord.

DAY 184

I Don't Feel Like Cleaning My Room

Adopt the same attitude as that of Christ Jesus. (Philippians 2:5)

Sometimes you just don't feel like cleaning your room. When your mom asks you to do something, you would rather do anything else. You might also feel annoyed, like *I just did that yesterday!* or *You do it yourself.* The Bible gives us advice for how to react when we feel like this. It says we're supposed to have the same attitude as Jesus. It also says we have to "make" our attitude like Jesus. That's because our first attitude is usually to complain and whine or to not do it. But in Christ, we can make our attitude better. God provides the strength and the heart to serve even when we don't feel like it. So the next time you have to do something you don't want to do, ask God to give you the attitude of Christ.

DAY 185

When You're Only the Little Sister

For he chose us in him, before the foundation of the world, to be holy and blameless in love before him. (Ephesians 1:4)

Have you ever been known as "____'s little sister"? All the teachers and everyone at church knows your older brother or sister, and you get tagged with being the little sister. It's frustrating when people assume things about you that aren't true just because you're in the same family. Don't stress. God sees you as someone completely separate from your siblings. He created you individually, with your exact personality and talents. He never sees you hiding behind your brother's or sister's shadow. He never forgets your name. You're also not forced to make the same choices as your older siblings. God wants you to get along with your whole family. He wants you to be friends with your siblings and have a great relationship, but He does not expect you to be exactly like them. So the next time you're labeled as the little sister, just smile, but know inside that you are totally unique to God, and He has an adventure for your life that's planned especially for you.

DAY 186

Sick of Being the Example—
A Big Sister Problem

"For I have given you an example, that you also should do just as I have done for you." (John 13:15)

Have you ever heard, "You need to set a good example for your younger sisters or brothers"? It's pretty annoying to always feel the pressure to set a good example. Actually, your younger siblings have a good example already, and it's not you. Jesus is more than willing to be the example of love, patience, serving, and honesty. The truth is, however, your younger siblings do look up to you. God has placed you in your family as an older sister for a reason. That doesn't mean you are the perfect example, but it means you need to point to the one who is perfect: Jesus. Your younger siblings copy the choices you make and the attitudes you have. You get the chance to teach them about Christ. So don't feel the pressure to be perfect; Jesus already did that. Just love God, and your siblings will see the difference it makes in your life. Your influence matters.

DAY 187

Fuzzy Pink and Charcoal Gray

If possible, as far as it depends on you,
live at peace with everyone. (Romans 12:18)

Do you have a sister who is the exact opposite of you in every way? Maybe you wonder how you even came from the same family. Did you know that God delights in our differences? He is so creative; He never makes cookie-cutter people. Your differences don't have to mean you fight all the time. In fact, opposites attract. When you have different talents and different hobbies, you can help each other be better. You just need to change your perspective. Stop seeing your differences as reasons to fight, and make peace. Encourage your sister and offer to help her. Look for ways that each of your strengths can work together. You don't have to like the same things to be friends. Pray for your sister and take steps to end the fighting. Your best friend just might live in the same house with you after all.

DAY 188

When You're Annoyed at Your Family

May the Lord cause you to increase and overflow with love
for one another and for everyone, just as we do for you.
(1 Thessalonians 3:12)

Is there someone in your family who knows exactly how to make you furious? He or she just walks in the room and you already feel annoyed. Although it sounds strange, being nice and serving them, can actually change your feelings toward them. Even if you don't feel like it, do something nice for the one who annoys you, without any expectation of a reward. Ask God for patience and an extra dose of love. He will give it to you. The beautiful thing about serving is that your feelings will follow your actions. The more you act loving toward someone, the more you actually start to love them. Dare to do something nice for someone in your family you really don't like. Even if you can't control your feelings, you can control your words and your actions by serving them. Then your feelings will follow.

DAY 189

Serving with Your Family

"For who is greater, the one at the table or the one serving? Isn't it the one at the table? But I am among you as the one who serves." (Luke 22:27)

Your family might be one of the greatest examples of Christ you can show the world. The world is desperate to see an example of a godly family. One way your family can make the most of your influence is to serve together. Look for ways to get involved in the community. You can work at a food bank or a clothes closet. You can rake a neighbor's yard or pick up trash on your street. You can donate old toys. The possibilities are endless. You can even talk to your church about a mission trip to another state. It's funny how you get closer together when you're serving side by side. Talk to your parents about serving together in your community. Even a small act to help someone else will bring your family closer together and shine the light of Christ in your neighborhood.

DAY 190

I'm Going to Kill My Sister

A fool's displeasure is known at once,
but whoever ignores an insult is sensible. (Proverbs 12:16)

When it comes to fighting with your family, are you a volcano, a sweeper, a waterfall, or a talker? In other words, when you get angry, do you explode with a temper, sweep away the problem like it never happened, cry like a waterfall, or talk so much that no one else can get a word in? Part of being in a family means learning how to deal with anger the right way. Instead of blowing up in a rage, take a few minutes to calm down. Don't avoid the problem, and deal with it soon. When you can speak calmly, explain your feelings. Then listen to the other point of view. Sometimes how you act in a disagreement is enough to help the other person calm down too. After discussing the problem, if you end up not getting your way, it's okay to be angry, but honor God in your anger. Everyone gets angry at their families. When you can be angry and still be respectful, you honor God and strengthen your family.

DAY 191

My Parents Don't Know Anything

Let everyone submit to the governing authorities,
since there is no authority except from God, and the
authorities that exist are instituted by God. (Romans 13:1)

Parents always seem to know everything until it comes to turning on their phones—then suddenly they need your help. It's funny how their brains sometimes go dark when it comes to anything with a power switch. Although you might think your parents don't know anything, they actually know a lot. Your parents have a lot of wisdom to give to you. They've lived many years and they've followed God a long time. They know how to protect you and how to give godly advice. When you have a problem, they are the best ones to go to because they love you more than anyone else. Are you taking advantage of your parents' wisdom? Do you listen when they teach you or do you tune them out? The next time you get a chance, really listen to your parents' teaching. Trust the decisions they make. Even if they don't know how to close an app on their phone, they have life wisdom that's more important. You'll be glad you listened.

Our God Is . . .

The only way to know our own worth is to know more about God. He is our Creator and our Savior. The more we know about Him, the more we love Him. This section takes our eyes off ourselves and puts them on God, exploring His character and attributes so we can be like Him.

DAY 192

Approachable

Therefore, let us approach the throne of grace with boldness, so that we may receive mercy and find grace to help us in time of need.
(Hebrews 4:16)

Have you ever been to a concert? How close were you able to get to the singers and musicians? Could you give them a hug? Eat a meal with them? Absolutely not. That's because in our culture, famous people create barriers around themselves. The more famous the star, the harder it is to get close to them. The most you could ever hope for is an autograph and a quick picture. The relationship is also one-sided. Fans love famous people, but famous people cannot love them back—at least not individually.

It is the exact opposite in the kingdom of God. The God of the universe—the most famous one who will ever be—is fully accessible to us because of Christ. We can come to Him anytime, day or night, and spend as much time with Him as we want. He not only tolerates us, He actually cares about us. Stop chasing famous people and realize that the most famous One is right in front of you, loving you, and ready to spend time with you.

DAY 193

Great

For the Lord is great and highly praised;
he is feared above all gods. (1 Chronicles 16:25)

Have you ever seen one of those pictures that's actually two pictures in one? If you look at it one way, it's an old lady, but if you see it another way, it's a young lady. It's all about your perspective. In the same way, our perspective impacts how we see the world. When we focus on the beauty and power of God, our problems seem small. When we focus on our problems, we get frustrated and overwhelmed. It's all about our perspective. Your perspective of God impacts whether or not you will trust Him. Praise the Lord in all things, and you will have His perspective on every choice, every problem, and every blessing.

DAY 194

Love

I pray that you, being rooted and firmly established in love, may be able to comprehend with all the saints what is the length and width, height and depth of God's love. (Ephesians 3:17–18)

God's love for you is more powerful than you realize. It covers you when you're in pain. It protects you when you're in trouble. His love is stronger than your worst fear and brighter than your darkest time. His love knows no limits. It doesn't depend on you—He loves you despite how you treat Him. God's love overcame the power of hell to find you. It created you, then it paid for you with arms stretched out on a cross. His love is gentle and patient, listening to you for hours and never getting bored. God loves you in the depths of who you are. Even a tiny glimpse of this love is enough to make us fall to our knees. Have you experienced this love—the love of God? Run to Him and know the only truly pure, selfless love that exists. His love is freedom. His love is joy. His love is waiting for you.

In the Beginning

In the beginning God created the heavens and the earth.
(Genesis 1:1)

Everything starts with God. He created the world by speaking it into existence. He is the start of every good thing, and He Himself has no beginning. When you remember that God is the Creator, you remember how big He is. Before there was any earth, sun, or stars there was God. Your God is the Creator of the world and your Creator. Whatever you face, He is big enough to handle it. He was around long before you were born and He will be alive for all eternity. You serve a big, powerful, mighty God who is worthy of our worship and able to handle everything we face. Worship Him today with your whole heart and trust Him with everything you face.

DAY 196

Our Anchor

We have this hope as an anchor for the soul, firm and secure. It enters the inner sanctuary behind the curtain. (Hebrews 6:19)

If you've ever taken a boat out to the middle of the ocean or a lake, you know how important the anchor is. If a boat isn't anchored or tied up, it will drift. Usually you don't even realize it, but when you look up, suddenly you're far away from where you want to be. The hope of Christ is the anchor of our souls. When we follow Christ, we have hope that keeps us from drifting spiritually. We don't have to stress out or come unglued when things go wrong. We trust in Him. When we don't cling to that hope, our lives will drift. What is your anchor? Anchor your life to the hope of Christ and you will stay close to God, even when everyone else is drifting.

DAY 197

Unchanging

Jesus Christ is the same yesterday, today, and forever.
(Hebrews 13:8)

Some things get old fast: stuff (don't expect me to carry last year's backpack), technology (nobody uses that anymore), music (that was so last month's song), and hair (do you really want the same haircut as your mom?). Some things change, and it hurts: When your parents get divorced, or your best friend finds a new best friend, or you have to move. Some things change, and it's just awkward: our bodies (enough said), our moods (can I get an "Amen"?).

In a world where nothing seems constant, we can be sure that one person will never change and that is Jesus. He is the exact same as He always was, and He will never change. His promises and His character will never move. We can cling to Him whenever we feel that change is happening too fast. He is our anchor in a storm of uncertainty. He is our sure thing. He will not change.

DAY 198

Giving

Every good and perfect gift is from above,
coming down from the Father of lights, who does not
change like shifting shadows. (James 1:17)

Sometimes we think of God as a mean reality show judge who constantly tells us how bad we are. God is nothing like that. Scripture says He is the giver of every single good and perfect gift in your life. Did something make you happy today? That was from God. Did you get to eat today and sleep with a roof over your head? That was from God. Do you have a friend you really trust? A blessing from God. The greatest gift of all was His Son, Jesus Christ, who died on a cross for you. Every good thing in your life came from God, and not by accident. He loves to bless you because He loves you. Concentrate on those blessings today. Create a heart of thanksgiving by focusing on what you do have instead of what you don't. You'll be amazed at how many blessings you recognize that maybe you never noticed before.

DAY 199

True Beauty

Out of the north he comes, shrouded in a golden glow;
awesome majesty surrounds him. (Job 37:22)

The world offers plenty of definitions of *beauty*. It describes how beauty should look, what it should wear, and what it should weigh. But the world's ideas of beauty are shallow. True beauty is found in God Himself. He is the source and the definition of beauty. We see God in the very person of Jesus, the most beautiful person who has ever lived. Don't misunderstand. Jesus wasn't an Abercrombie model. His physical appearance wasn't dazzling. His life, however, made Him beautiful. He was the picture of gentleness, peace, and joy. He had no fear, no anxiety, and no hate. His presence was so full of joy that He was a magnet to people. And the most beautiful picture of His love for us happened on the cross, where He died in our place. I know every girl wants to be beautiful. It's what our culture values most about girls. But what if you sought the kind of radiant beauty of our Savior? You can have it. The more time you spend with God, the more you will reflect the beauty of the Savior—a beauty deeper, purer, and sweeter than anything the world can make.

DAY 200

Creator

*Do you not know? Have you not heard? The L*ORD *is the everlasting God, the Creator of the whole earth. He never becomes faint or weary; there is no limit to his understanding. (Isaiah 40:28)*

People have built some pretty cool things—skyscrapers, pyramids, bridges, roller coasters. But nothing compares to what God has created. He is the Creator of everything we see and everything in existence. He made water, trees, flowers, and the air we breathe. He made the Grand Canyon, the magnificent waterfalls, the planets, and the sun. Those same hands also formed us. He made every cell in our body, every bone, and every organ. The God we serve is the greatest Creator, the most amazing builder of all time. There is no limit to His imagination. Worship Him today for all He has made. Today, notice His creation all around you, even when you look in a mirror, and give Him praise.

DAY 201

Jealous

"Do not make an idol for yourself, whether in the shape of anything in the heavens above or on the earth below or in the waters under the earth. Do not bow in worship to them, and do not serve them; for I, the Lord your God, am a jealous God, punishing the children for the fathers' iniquity, to the third and fourth generations of those who hate me." (Exodus 20:4–5)

Has one of your friends ever been jealous of you? It's not a good feeling. They want what you have and can't be happy when you succeed. Scripture says God is jealous over us, and it's a totally different kind of jealousy. He's not jealous of us; He's jealous for us. We were created to be in a relationship with God, and when anything threatens that relationship, He is jealous. He loves you so deeply that He hates the sin and the distractions that keep you from Him. No one will ever love you as passionately and as fully as God. He will fight for you and He will run after you. The God of the universe is jealous over you. Let that kind of love capture your heart.

DAY 202

Satisfying

You satisfy me as with rich food; my mouth
will praise you with joyful lips. (Psalm 63:5)

Every girl wants to be satisfied. TV, magazines, YouTube, and movies offer thousands of things that promise to satisfy: trendy clothes, the perfect body, popularity, true love, fame, lots of money. You don't have to look far to realize that none of those things bring satisfaction. In fact, the more of the world's promises you believe, the worse you feel. But there is a source of true satisfaction that never goes away. God can satisfy every one of your needs. He is able to fulfill you totally and completely. When you desire Him above everything else, He will not disappoint. What are you hoping will satisfy you? What are your deepest dreams and longings? Come to God with your whole heart, and He will meet you with open arms.

DAY 203

Patient

*The L{.sc ORD} is gracious and compassionate, slow to anger
and great in faithful love. (Psalm 145:8)*

Some teachers are really mean. They never smile, they yell all the time, and you secretly wonder if they ride a broomstick home from school. No matter how hard you try, you just can't do anything right for these teachers. Some people see God like this—as an angry teacher who's constantly upset at you. But the Bible tells us that God is exactly the opposite. Our God is slow to anger. He is full of grace and compassion. When you mess up and disappoint Him, He is quick to forgive and to help you up. He is quick to celebrate when you do something right and slow to be angry when you mess up. If you've been thinking of God as an angry teacher, change your perspective. He does not operate out of anger. When you fall, He doesn't hold out a stick to whack you; He offers a hand to help you up. Trust His forgiveness and His compassion.

DAY 204

On Your Side

We know that all things work together for the good of those who love God, who are called according to His purpose. (Romans 8:28)

You know the arcade game where the moles pop up from their holes and you whack them back down again? Have you ever felt like God was playing that game with us, like every time we do something wrong, God whacks us on the head in anger? One of the most powerful truths you can learn about God is that He is on your side! He is your Father and your Creator. He wants you to walk with Him, and He wants you to experience all the blessings and joy that can only be found in His presence. When bad things happen, God is not punishing you. He's giving you the chance to run into His arms. He is working the hard times into something that's actually good for you. God delights when you make good choices and honor Him with your life. When you mess up, you will have consequences, but He will forgive you and help you get back on track. Trust Him when things go right and when things are hard, and He will work His plan in your life.

DAY 205

Near

As for me, God's presence is my good. I have made the Lord God
my refuge, so I can tell about all you do. (Psalm 73:28)

He's closer than the air you breathe. He's more real than anything you can touch or see. God is near to you. One of the biggest lies you can buy is that God is far away from you. God is never far from you. No matter how you feel at the moment, God is closer to you than you know. He loves you so much, and He is involved in everything you do. He knows your problems, your fears, your joys, and your very thoughts. God does not leave when you mess up. He doesn't walk away when you have an ugly cry (you know the one when your faces gets red and your eyes get puffy). He's always close to you, so draw close to Him. Invite Him into your day, your thoughts, and your feelings. Whisper your heart to Him; He delights to hear your voice. God just wants you, exactly as you are. He will never leave you or forsake you. Trust Him.

DAY 206

Strong

*The LORD reigns! He is robed in majesty;
the LORD is robed, enveloped in strength. The world
is firmly established; it cannot be shaken. (Psalm 93:1)*

Words like *kind*, *gentle*, *compassionate*, and *patient* are usually given to a nice old grandpa, not a mighty warrior. But did you know that, along with being kind, gentle, and patient, our God is also strong and fierce. He commands the strongest storms and the entire universe bows to Him. He is able to destroy any and every enemy He chooses. How do you need God's strength in your life today? What enemy is threatening you? The Lord is strong enough to defeat it. With Him, you can face any battle. As you think of God, remember that although He is merciful, forgiving, and gentle, He is also the strongest warrior and capable of defeating all the problems that rise up against you.

DAY 207

Your Father

God in his holy dwelling is a father of the fatherless and a champion of widows. (Psalm 68:5)

There are many different kinds of dads. Some dads are great fathers who love and protect their daughters. Some dads are angry. Some dads are just not there. No matter what kind of dad you have on the earth, your heavenly Father God is the best dad you will ever have. The God of the universe is your Creator, your Protector, your Savior, but He is also your Dad. God thinks of you as His daughter, and He loves you just as a daughter. He is never absent, never overreacts, and never lets you down. He will provide for you. He will always come to you when you need Him. You can tell Him anything and trust Him with anything.

Not Finished with You Yet

I am sure of this, that he who started a good work in you will carry it on to completion until the day of Christ Jesus. (Philippians 1:6)

Yet Lord, you are our Father; we are the clay, and you are our potter; we all are the work of your hands. (Isaiah 64:8)

Have you ever started a project like drawing, sewing, or painting pottery and hated what you were doing? Usually when we get frustrated with our work, we throw it away and start over. We need a blank canvas or a fresh sheet of paper. Thankfully, God doesn't react like this at all. The Bible says that we are clay in the hands of our Father. What happens when the clay gets a chip or starts to look ugly? What happens when we are selfish, talk back to our parents, or bully our siblings? Does God just throw us away? Not at all. He will never throw you away no matter what. He doesn't give up on you; He just keeps working on you. God will finish what He started when He saved you. He longs for you to look more like His Son, Jesus, every day, and He will smooth out every broken, scratched part of you until that happens.

DAY 209

Your Greatest Reward

But I myself said: I have labored in vain, I have spent my strength for nothing and futility; yet my vindication is with the LORD, and my reward is with my God. (Isaiah 49:4)

Have you ever done something nice for your family and no one noticed? Maybe you set the table, took out the trash, or cleaned your room and no one even bothered to thank you. Sometimes you feel like the same thing is happening in your walk with God. Maybe you feel like you've been trying to do the right thing, but things just aren't getting better. You wonder if God has forgotten about you or if the Christian life really makes a difference. In these frustrating times, trust God. The Bible promises that our faithfulness will be rewarded. Sometimes those rewards are physical blessings. Sometimes those rewards are spiritual blessings like joy, peace, and kindness. And sometimes, like in this Bible verse, God Himself is our reward. Sometimes being close to Him is our reward, and that is actually the most encouraging reward you can experience. So when you've worked hard for God and you don't really see any blessings, just trust that your God has not forgotten you. He sees every good work and He will bless you, most of all with Himself—the greatest blessing possible.

Our God Will . . .

After we know who God is, we need to know what He can do. Our God is powerful and able to work great things in our lives. This section focuses on just a few things God wants to do in our lives when we trust in Him.

DAY
210

Forgive

Iniquities overwhelm me; only you can atone for our rebellions. (Psalm 65:3)

Have you ever accidentally broken something in a store? Your parents get really mad because they have to pay for it, and then they usually make you pay for it. You have to replace what's broken. In Christ, we can't pay for our own sins. We can't do enough good works to cancel out the bad. God alone can pay the price for our sins. He is faithful to forgive. When Jesus died on the cross, He took the punishment for our sins. He was perfect, so He was the only acceptable sacrifice. In Him, we have forgiveness. Your Father offers you forgiveness for your sins. In Christ, you can have total confidence that your sins are paid for and you are forgiven.

DAY
211

Confide in Us

*The secret counsel of the LORD is for those who fear him,
and he reveals his covenant to them. (Psalm 25:14)*

When an adult trusts you with a secret, you feel pretty important. You know they believe in you enough to handle something big without betraying them. When you seek God and love Him most, He will entrust you with things. He will show you things in His Word that not everyone understands. He will add to your wisdom and understanding of Him, as much as you want to have. The secret to God's wisdom is to love Him and obey His Word. When God has your heart, you will have His wisdom. If you want to understand the hidden things of God, love Him. He will show you more of Himself and His truths every day.

Energize

Those who trust in the Lord will renew their strength;
they will soar on wings like eagles; they will run and
not become weary; they will walk and not faint. (Isaiah 40:31)

A lot of things claim to give us energy in the day: coffee, sugar, food, music. Even Red Bull claims to give us wings. When you're feeling tired and drained, there is only one source of true energy—trusting in the Lord. When you call to Him and seek His presence, He will renew your strength. The Bible says you will soar on wings like eagles and run without getting tired. Obviously that doesn't mean God can make you run an instant marathon, but He can give you endless energy in your spiritual life. When you're burned out on doing good, or you feel like the fruit of the Spirit in your life is turning sour, God can revive you. There is no other source of spiritual energy than His presence. If you need a spiritual energy drink, God can give it to you. Rest in Him, trust Him, and He will strengthen you.

DAY 213

Carry You

"I will be the same until your old age, and I will bear you up when you turn gray. I have made you, and I will carry you; I will bear and rescue you." (Isaiah 46:4)

Sometimes every little girl needs her daddy to carry her. When she's hurt or tired or just wants to play and have fun, a good dad's arms are perfect. Whether or not your earthly dad carried you, your heavenly Father will carry you. You can come to His arms for any reason, and He will lift you up and hold you close. He loves you more than you could possibly imagine. With Him, you are safe and you are unconditionally loved. Scripture says He made us and He will carry us. When you're feeling brokenhearted, exhausted, or just lonely, let your Father's arms pick you up. He made you. He knows you. And He will carry you.

DAY 214

Make New

Therefore, if anyone is in Christ, he is a new creation; the old has passed away, and see, the new has come! (2 Corinthians 5:17)

When a creepy caterpillar comes out of a cocoon, it doesn't come out a prettier, more colorful caterpillar. It's a totally new creation. A butterfly doesn't scoot along with its face in the dirt; it feels the wind under it's wings and it flies. When you come to Christ, God doesn't just make a better version of your old self; He gives you a totally new self. He replaces your old desires, thoughts, and plans with His desires, His thoughts, and His plans. He gives you new confidence, new peace, and new joy. He gives you His presence. When you are in Christ, you no longer have to fear the same things the world fears. He loves you so much, and He refuses to leave you like He found you. Take joy that God has transformed you, and you are a new creation in Him.

DAY 215

Bless

Take delight in the Lᴏʀᴅ, and he will give you your heart's desires. (Psalm 37:4)

God loves to bless you. He loves to surprise you with gifts of His presence throughout the day. Scripture says when you delight in the Lord, He will give you what your heart desires. That's because when you draw close to God and spend time with Him, you will desire the exact same things He desires for you. You will love the things He loves and hate the things He hates. What blessings do you see all around you? Ask God to give you eyes to see the surprise blessings He has planned for you today. Find joy in the Lord and He will bless you more than you could ever imagine.

DAY 216

Hear

If we know that he hears whatever we ask, we know that we have what we have asked of him. (1 John 5:15)

Have you ever tried to have a conversation with someone who's texting? It's so annoying. They hear about half of what you say, then bury their face in the screen to text some more. You can be confident that God never texts when you're talking to Him. He's never distracted. He knows the sound of your voice. He hears every word you speak. He also delights to give you what you ask for. When you ask for something that's in His will and lines up with His purpose, He will give it to you. When God withholds something from you, you can be confident that He has a greater purpose. He loves you so much, and He loves to hear you speak to Him. There is no topic off-limits and nothing you can't ask for. Talk to God and He will always hear.

DAY 217

Save

Once you were alienated and hostile in your minds expressed in your evil actions. But now he has reconciled you by his physical body through his death, to present you holy, faultless, and blameless before him. (Colossians 1:21–22)

You know those before-and-after pictures that magazines use to sell stuff? The "before" picture is always a sad, gloomy picture of a girl with tons of zits and no friends. Then she used a certain brand of makeup and all her problems went away. The "after" picture is a beautiful, happy girl with tons of friends and cool clothes. In Christ, you have a before-and-after picture, only it's real and not used to sell something. Before you came to Christ, you had no hope. You bought all the lies of the world, and you were a slave to your own selfishness. Then God changed everything. He gave you joy, peace, love, and security. That kind of before-and after-picture lets the world know that God is real and that He really changes you. Your lost friends need Jesus to change their lives, not a new kind of makeup or a new wardrobe. You have the answer they need, and your life is the proof they're looking for.

DAY 218

Give Courage

"Haven't I commanded you: be strong and courageous?
Do not be afraid or discouraged, for the LORD your God is
with you wherever you go." (Joshua 1:9)

Courage doesn't come from physical strength. It doesn't come from beauty or intelligence or money. True courage comes from the Lord. Courage is the ability to stand before something scary or intimidating and not back down. It's the power to make the right choice, even when it means you'll be teased. God is willing and able to fill your heart with great courage. God tells us "do not be afraid" because He knows we usually are afraid. He knows that we struggle with fear. He alone can melt away that fear because He is with us. Ask God to give you courage to live for Him. Even when you feel afraid, trust God more than the fear. Your God is mighty and powerful. He will never fail you. Cling to the courage He gives you so you can see Him do amazing things in your life.

DAY 219

Keep His Promises

For every one of God's promises is "Yes" in him.
Therefore, through him we also say "Amen" to the glory of God.
(2 Corinthians 1:20)

We hear the word *no* a lot every day. "No, you can't wear that." "No, you can't go there." "No, you can't eat that." "No, you can't say that." Sometimes it can feel like God says no a lot too. Although He does give us boundaries for our protection, God says yes a whole lot more than He says no. God gives us hundreds of promises that are all for our blessings. Yes, we can have forgiveness. Yes, we can have true joy, peace, and love. Yes, we can come to God whenever we want. Yes, we can have all our needs met by His riches. If we focus on the "yeses" of God, the "nos" don't seem like that big of a deal. God delights to give us blessings, and only gives us because He loves us. What are the "yeses" of God you are thankful for today?

DAY 220

Pierce the Darkness

For you were once darkness, but now you are light in the Lord.
Live as children of light—for the fruit of the light consists of
all goodness, righteousness, and truth. (Ephesians 5:8–9)

Light destroys darkness. When you turn on the light in a room, everything dark goes away. As followers of Christ, that's how we live. You are the light of Christ in the world. When you enter a room, you bring His light with you. You shine His light in a pitch-black place. Whether it's on your sports team, in your school, or in your neighborhood, the world needs to see that light. Be different. Speak differently and act differently. This verse says that the light of Christ results in all goodness. The light can't help but chase away darkness. When you live as the light of Christ, you will shine His love wherever you go and whatever you do.

DAY 221

Do the Work

Be satisfied with what you have, for he himself has said,
I will never leave you or abandon you. (Hebrews 13:5)

Have you ever had to do a group project for school and you got stuck in a terrible group? One student never comes to school; another one is lazy. The other student tries to help, but he just doesn't have good ideas. Guess who ends up doing all the work? You! Then the whole group gets a good grade because of your hard work. When you obey God with your life, you never have to wonder if He's going to abandon you. He always comes through. Whether it's a tough situation with a friend or a tense time at home, He is by your side. Honestly, God is the one who does the work. It's never a partnership with Him, it's just Him doing the work through you. When you stay close to God, He will accomplish things through you like loving your enemy, speaking kind words, and sharing the gospel. When you follow Christ with your life, He does all the work and you get all the blessings. It's a pretty sweet arrangement.

Going to Battle

Every day a battle rages for your heart, your attention, and your worship. As girls who follow Christ, we must be strong against our enemy—the devil. This section teaches us how to be strong in Christ and how to fight with weapons that matter.

DAY
222

Dressed and Ready:
The Armor of God

*Finally, be strengthened by the Lord and by his vast strength.
Put on the full armor of God so that you can stand
against the schemes of the devil. (Ephesians 6:10–11)*

When you play a sport, you have to wear certain protective gear. Depending on your sport, you might need a knee brace, a batting helmet, shin guards, or a glove. Soldiers, police officers, and firemen wear extreme protective gear because they go into dangerous situations. As followers of Christ, the Bible commands us to put on our armor. It's invisible to the eye, but it's there. Like a spiritual bulletproof shield, the armor of God protects against the attacks of the enemy. God's Word describes protection for our mind, our hearts, and our feet. It also describes our sword. We'll study this armor more in the coming days. It's time for girls to stop trying to face the world's temptations with no armor. We need the armor of Christ.

DAY 223

Belt of Truth

Stand, therefore, with truth like a belt around your waist,
righteousness like armor on your chest. (Ephesians 6:14)

A girl's got to have a cute belt. Belts are a super easy way to add color and texture to a dress or shirt. When the Bible tells us to buckle the belt of truth around our waist, it's not talking about a bright turquoise accessory to accent your brown sundress. The belt of truth is like a belt in that it circles us. It wraps itself all the way around our lives, protecting us from lies. When you study God's Word and know God, you have the belt of truth. Then when someone tries to convince you to disobey God, you aren't fooled because you know truth. In John 14:6 Jesus said, "I am the way, the truth, and the life." When you know Christ more, you know what's true and you can spot a fake. So buckle that belt of truth around your life, and you will be strong in the Lord.

DAY 224

Feet of Peace

And your feet sandaled with readiness for the gospel of peace.
(Ephesians 6:15)

Shoes are a girl's best friend. Heels, flats, sandals, Toms, flip-flops, or jellies, they just make a girl feel good. Your shoes say a lot about your personality too. The Bible says that one important piece of armor we need to put on every day is the shoes of peace. It sounds strange to put on shoes of peace when we're talking about going to battle. How can peace and battle exist at the same time? The peace of Christ is powerful. When you put on the shoes of peace, it means that you stand in the peace of Christ. His gospel of peace is your foundation. Nothing the world throws at you can shake you. The world is stressed out, worried, and full of anxiety. In the presence of God, all worry melts away. When you put on your spiritual armor, remember that you have the peace of Christ in your life and you stand on it in complete security.

DAY 225

The Armor That Guards Your Heart

Stand, therefore, with truth like a belt around your waist, righteousness like armor on your chest. (Ephesians 6:14)

When police officers wear a bulletproof vest, they don't wear it on their feet or their arms. Their vest covers the most important part of the body, the source of life itself—the heart. The armor of righteousness on your chest does the same thing for us spiritually. When you came to Christ, you were not holy or righteous. You were covered with sin and selfishness and in rebellion against God. Then Jesus, who was righteous, put His holiness on you and made you clean. His righteousness is applied to your life, and you are righteous before God. That's why it guards your heart. Through Christ, your heart belongs to God. He is your first love. When you love Him with your whole heart, you are protected against the enemy. Other loves, like popularity, insecurity, or stuff, can't compete with your love for Christ. You put on the armor of righteousness by letting God have your heart and by becoming more like Him every day. Your heart is safe when it's in the hands of God.

DAY 226

When Arrows Fall to the Ground

In every situation take up the shield of faith with which you can extinguish all the flaming arrows of the evil one. (Ephesians 6:16)

If you've ever had a snowball fight, then you know how important a shield is. You need something, a tree or a snow fort, to hide behind when the icy snow starts flying toward you. A shield keeps you from getting hit. In Christ, your shield is your faith. It's your trust that God is who He says He is and that He can do what He says He can do. When you trust Him, no arrow of the enemy can hit you. The enemy's arrows are specifically designed to target your weaknesses. He lies to you with promises of popularity, beauty, and freedom. He launches arrows that try to get you to hate your parents, be mean to your siblings, and gossip about your friends. The shield of faith makes those arrows fall to the ground. Cling to the shield of faith when you feel attacked. It will protect you from every arrow.

Why Helmet Hair Is Beautiful

Finally brothers and sisters, whatever is true, whatever is honorable, whatever is just, whatever is pure, whatever is lovely, whatever is commendable—if there is any moral excellence and if there is anything praiseworthy—dwell on these things. (Philippians 4:8)

Girls usually don't like to wear helmets because they really mess up our hair, but there are certain times we just have to do it. Riding a bicycle, playing paintball, bungee jumping, and skateboarding all demand we cover our heads. Why wear a helmet? Because it protects an important part of your body (not your beautiful hair)—your brain. Did you know that God demands we put on a kind of helmet every day? He calls it the helmet of salvation—it's our godly thoughts. When we focus our thoughts on God and the sacrifice of Christ in our lives, it acts as a helmet to our thinking. All kinds of evil and discouraging thoughts attack you every day, thoughts of anger, jealousy, insecurity, and fear. Every girl knows the power our thoughts have over us. When you put on the helmet of godly thoughts, you push away the distractions and the thoughts that tear you down. Then you can make choices that come from godly thoughts, not worldly ones. Our thoughts will either push us close to God or drive us away from Him. That's why a girl's gotta have her helmet.

DAY 228

Ready, Aim, Worship!

About midnight Paul and Silas were praying and singing hymns to God, and the prisoners were listening to them. Suddenly there was such a violent earthquake that the foundations of the jail were shaken, and immediately all the doors were opened, and everyone's chains came loose. (Acts 16:25–26)

Sometimes the most powerful thing you can do is worship God. We tend to think that singing songs to God is cute and fun, but that it doesn't actually help us out of the mess we're in. Actually, it does. For Paul and Silas, worshipping God caused their chains to shatter and the doors to their prison came open. When you worship God, you might not see any chains break physically, but you will feel the chains of fear, insecurity, loneliness, and pain shatter to the floor. What problem are you facing? Worship God. What joy are you experiencing? Worship God. What are you thankful for? Worship Him. When you praise Him, you are using a powerful weapon against the enemy. Watch what happens in your life when you worship God every day.

DAY
229

Never Fight Alone

"The Lord your God is among you, a warrior who saves. He will rejoice over you with gladness. He will be quiet in his love. He will delight in you with singing." (Zephaniah 3:17)

Have you ever tried to stand up to a bully thinking there was a crowd of people behind you? Then you realize, you're the only one! It's pretty discouraging. Scripture tells us that God never deserts us in our moment of need. In fact, He is the warrior beside us who saves us. No matter what problem you face, no matter how big or small it seems, you do not have to face it alone. Your God stands beside you. And that's more important than any number of friends. What do you need to face with God at your side? Fight it together.

DAY 230

Enemy in Disguise

Be sober-minded, be alert. Your adversary the devil is prowling around like a roaring lion, looking for anyone he can devour.
(1 Peter 5:8)

The most dangerous enemy is the one you never see coming. Girls, we have a real enemy seeking to destroy us. Satan wants to destroy our confidence, our modesty, our trust in God. He seeks to wreck our friendships and our relationships with our parents. His plan is to do everything possible to distract us from the presence of God. We don't have to be afraid, but we must be on guard. What music are you listening to? What movies do you watch? What do you read online? Who's advice are you following? Are you putting things in your mind to draw you close to God? We have to be on guard against the enemy and fill our minds with the truth of God. The safest place to be is in a strong relationship with Him. Seek the Lord, and the enemy will not be able to get to you. You will recognize every attack the enemy throws at you, and you can fight back with the truth of God's Word.

DAY 231

Not a Powder-Puff Sword

For the word of God is living and effective and sharper than any double-edged sword, penetrating as far as the separation of soul and spirit, joints and marrow. It is able to judge the thoughts and intentions of the heart. (Hebrews 4:12)

Some girls go into battle carrying a hairbrush and try to swing it at the enemy. Some carry a mirror. Others carry a tube of lipstick or a cute pair of shoes. While these items aren't bad, they are useless in a battle. The Bible says there is only one sword, and that is the Word of God. When you learn Scripture, you have a powerful weapon in your hands. Scripture can be used to fight off a negative attitude. You can use it to strike temptation. You can slice away the lies the enemy tries to throw at you about true beauty and confidence. So memorize it, write it down, and put it on your mirror or your locker. Encourage a friend with it. Become a well-trained fighter. When you use the Bible as a sword, you are a powerful warrior against anything the world can throw at you. So while other girls try to use their beauty, popularity, fashion, or intelligence, you cling to the Word of God, and it will not fail you.

DAY 232

Hear Me Pray

Happy are the people whose strength is in you,
whose hearts are set on pilgrimage. (Psalm 84:5)

When you hear the words *strong woman*, what do you picture? Maybe you see someone who is physically strong, great at sports. Maybe you see someone who is confident, beautiful with a loud personality. Maybe you pictured someone with lots of money or someone famous or popular. These kinds of strength are great for a while, but they will all fail eventually. The only source of strength that will never fail is found in Christ. He alone can make us strong from the inside out. A girl who finds her strength in Christ does not easily cave to temptation. She does the right thing, even when no one is looking. She speaks kindly, even when someone really annoys her. That kind of strength can only come from God. What kind of strength are you seeking? Ask God to be your strength, and see what kind of spiritual muscle He can build in you.

DAY 233

Step Aside, He's Got This One

For I do not trust in my bow, and my sword does not bring me victory. (Psalm 44:6)

The Lord will rescue me from every evil work and will bring me safely into his heavenly kingdom. To him be the glory forever and ever! Amen. (2 Timothy 4:18)

Have you ever played a video game and died on the very same place a hundred times? It's really frustrating. When that happens, we usually just hand the control to our friend, brother, or sister to get us past that part. It's always easy when someone else fights for us. In life, sometimes God wants you to step aside so He can fight your battle for you. Is there a situation that you just can't get through? Have you tried a hundred times, but nothing is working? Maybe it's time to stop trying to fix it yourself and step back so God can work. Your own words and your wisdom will fail, but God is fully able to do the work Himself. Do not worry, and do not be afraid. Just hand the problem to God and stay close to Him. He will bring you through.

DAY 234

The Only Story That Has Power

Because our gospel did not come to you in word only,
but also in power, in the Holy Spirit, and with full assurance.
(1 Thessalonians 1:5)

We hear stories all the time. Our teachers read them to us, our grandparents tell them, and we watch stories lived out in movies. Only one story, however, has power—the story of Jesus. The gospel is the only story that has the power to change lives. Every time you share Christ with someone, you tell a story that comes with great power. You never have to be embarrassed or shy to talk about Jesus. No matter how people respond, the gospel is the only way to salvation. It's not just words. It's not just a cute tale like you read in your favorite book. It is the life-changing power of God. Share the gospel and you tell a story with the power to save.

When the Odds Are Ever in Your Favor

Then Asa cried out to the Lord his God: "Lord, there is no one besides you to help the mighty and those without strength. Help us, Lord our God, for we depend on you, and in your name we have come against this large army. Lord, you are our God." (2 Chronicles 14:11)

When was the last time you felt really outnumbered? Maybe it was an actual game where your team had a couple of weak players and the other team had some real athletes. Maybe you felt outnumbered when friends or siblings ganged up on you. When you're stressed out or have a lot of problems, you can also feel outnumbered. In the verse above, Asa tells God, "We depend on you." When you have God on your side, you are never outnumbered. In fact, He likes to do His best work when He gets all the credit instead of you. He loves to step in and save the day. Call out to the Lord when you feel overwhelmed or outnumbered, and He will come to your rescue.

DAY
236

Stronger Than the Wind

*Therefore, my dear brothers and sisters, be steadfast, immovable,
always excelling in the Lord's work, because you know that your
labor in the Lord is not in vain. (1 Corinthians 15:58)*

Not many things can stand strong against a hurricane. Even the sturdiest building collapses if the wind is strong enough. Girls, in this world, a fierce wind wants to knock you over. This wind is made up of greed, selfishness, insecurity, fear, anger, sexual temptation, gossip, and immodesty. Everywhere you look, girls fall to this powerful wind. The only way you can stand strong against this wind is through Christ. He is stronger than the strongest winds of the world. When you cling to Him, you don't have to be swept away by the world. He will give you joy, peace, purpose, and security. When He is your foundation, you will not be moved. You don't have to love the things the world loves, but you can find your joy and confidence in Christ. Stand strong with the arms of the Lord holding you fast. No winds of the world will be able to knock you down.

DAY 237

Clueless

We are powerless before this vast number that comes to fight against us. We do not know what to do, but we look to you.
(2 Chronicles 20:12)

Sometimes you just don't know what to do in a situation. Maybe a friendship has you caught in the middle or a big decision is weighing you down. I love the verse that says, "We do not know what to do, but we look to you." When you don't know what to do, when you're stuck with a tough choice or you are overwhelmed with a heavy heart, look to God. Focus your attention on Him and He will guide you to His will. There is no decision too small or too big for God's wisdom. He loves you, and He will direct you to the best choice.

DAY 238

When the Battle Isn't Yours to Fight

He said, "Listen carefully, all Judah and you inhabitants of Jerusalem, and King Jehoshaphat. This is what the LORD says: 'Do not be afraid or discouraged because of this vast number, for the battle is not yours, but God's.'" (2 Chronicles 20:15)

Have you ever rescued your little brother or sister from a bully? A big, bad five-year-old thinks he can push everyone around, then you walk up to him. Suddenly the mean bully is silent. All of a sudden, he's shaking in his Spider-Man shoes. He's not about to mess with your brother or sister when you're around.

When it comes to the problems we face every day, it's all about who's standing over your shoulder. Sometimes God wants us to fight the battles with His strength, but sometimes He just wants us to step aside so He can deal with the problem. What issues are you facing? Remember that God is always standing right beside you, and you never have to be afraid.

DAY
239

Patience Is Better Than Power

*Patience is better than power, and controlling
one's emotions, than capturing a city. (Proverbs 16:32)*

In our world, power is everything. Getting ahead is all about how strong you are, how smart you are, how rich you are, and how many people you can control. In reality, though, people who look the most powerful on the outside are often the weakest. God says that patience is better than power. That seems completely backward. Since when is a patient old granny more powerful than an angry warrior? It's true. Patience is the ability to control your emotions and your impulses in order to wait for something better. It's the ability to avoid rushing into a stupid situation because you see the bigger picture. Patience waits on God. Power waits on yourself. Power trusts in your strength. Patience trusts in God's strength. God is stronger every time. So the next time you have a chance to use power to get what you want, back off. Be patient instead, and trust God to do something greater than your own strength could ever accomplish.

Brave

Around every corner we find something to fear. Christ wants to crush those fears with the power of His presence. This sections helps us discover the courage we already have in Him.

DAY
240

Nothing to Fear

Therefore, we may boldly say: The Lord is my helper; I will not be afraid. What can man do to me? (Hebrews 13:6)

There are plenty of reasons to be afraid in our world. Every day we hear about something scary or sad happening that strikes fear in our hearts. In Christ, fear doesn't have to weigh us down. When God is on your side, nothing can come against you. The safest place you can be is inside the shadow of His wings. It's true that sometimes bad things happen, but God is with you every second and gives you all the tools you need to get through it. Without Christ, we have plenty to be afraid of. But when we know Him, we have peace the world doesn't understand. Christ Himself is our rock, and we are His children. And nothing can take that away from us.

DAY 241

Spirit of Power

For God has not given us a spirit of fearfulness, but one of power, love, and sound judgment. (2 Timothy 1:7)

It takes great courage for a girl to live for God. Everywhere you turn, you have the chance to disobey God. Often when you follow God, that means you have to turn your back on what everyone else is doing. Following Christ is not for weak girls. You can be confident that God is on your side, cheering you on. He did not give you a spirit of fear, but a spirit of power, a spirit of love, and a spirit of wisdom. The closer you get to God and the more time you spend with Him, the more fear melts away. God longs to give you the courage you need to stand for Him. He will make you into a courageous girl after His own heart. What if you love God, but you're still afraid? That's okay. God will help you through the fear. He loves you so much, and He will give you everything you need to follow Him with boldness.

DAY 242

Small Job, Big Courage

Stephen, full of grace and power, was performing great wonders and signs among the people. (Acts 6:8)

Stephen was a courageous follower of Christ who had great power in his life. You might think he was a pastor or a disciple, but he wasn't. Stephen looked after the little old ladies in the church. The early church leaders needed someone to care for the widows because it was taking up too much of their time. It was probably a job not many would have wanted, but Stephen volunteered. Maybe you don't feel like your job is very important in the body of Christ right now. Maybe you don't feel like babysitting your little brother or sister is a super important job. But sometimes God takes the little things, and He makes them matter a whole lot. Sometimes the truly courageous people are people who do ordinary things for the glory of God. Do you have courage to live for Christ in the small things? You never know how God will use you for His glory.

The Roar of the Lioness

The wicked flee when no one is pursuing them,
but the righteous are as bold as a lion. (Proverbs 28:1)

Nothing scares a lioness. Female lions are great hunters and kill most of the food for their families. They have scissor-like teeth that shred their prey, and their roar can be heard from five miles away. The Bible says when you follow Christ, you are as bold as a lion. You don't have to fear anything the world fears. Your God has defeated every enemy that could possibly attack. Nothing has the power to overtake you. You are no longer chained to sin or a slave to your own selfishness. It's time we stopped letting the fears of the world make us afraid. Girls who follow God are as strong as lions. We can live boldly for God, obeying His Word, and loving other people. Instead of running from your fears, stop and roar the Word of God. When you have the confidence of a lion, nothing can shake you.

Source for lion facts: http://www.sciencekids.co.nz/sciencefacts/animals/lion.html.

DAY 244

Unshakable Confidence

So don't throw away your confidence,
which has a great reward. (Hebrews 10:35)

More than a million dollars, I think most girls would rather have confidence. Confidence is knowing and accepting who you are and liking yourself. In Christ, you can have absolute, complete confidence in who you are. Christ-centered confidence starts with knowing who God is. When you know how amazing God is, then you start to understand His love for you. The fact that a great and powerful God loves you and made you is enough to bring confidence to even the most insecure girl. Not only did God make you, but He wants to be involved in your life. He gave His own Son to have a relationship with you. He has blessed you with a combination of gifts and talents that no one else has. He believes in you and has a purpose for your life. When you're feeling bad about yourself, cling to the confidence of Christ. In Him, you are absolutely beautiful and capable of doing great things for His name. Live, breathe, and sleep in the unshakable confidence that comes from knowing Jesus Christ as Lord.

DAY 245

Breaking Fear

He will not fear bad news; his heart is confident,
trusting in the Lord. (Psalm 112:7)

In this world, we have a lot to fear. Every day we hear about violence, disease, and evil people hurting others. We hear about natural disasters that destroy homes, not to mention the worries in our own lives like parents losing their jobs, bullies, or the stress of school. Fear is enough to make us want to lock ourselves in our rooms. In Christ, however, the fear of bad news can have no power over you. When you trust in God, you don't have to be weighed down by worry or fear. You trust God and know that nothing will happen that He won't guide you through. Even if something bad happens, you don't have to be defeated. You don't have to worry about something happening to you or someone you love. What fears weigh you down? Take them to God, and let Him replace that fear with His unshakable fear and confidence.

DAY 246

All About Jesus

Jesus is the Son of God and the perfect visual example for us to follow. To follow Christ, we have to know about how He lived. This section deals with who Jesus was, things Jesus did, and how we can look more like Him.

Help for Visual Learners

Therefore, be imitators of God,
as dearly loved children. (Ephesians 5:1)

Some people can learn just by hearing something explained one time. Others—called visual learners—need to see a picture of how to do it. Just hearing it or reading it isn't enough. They need an example. The Bible helps all kinds of learners live the Christian life. Jesus is the picture of how to live. For those of us who need a visual example, Jesus shows us exactly how to love, how to pray, how to live, and how to forgive. He shows us how to treat people and how to have patience. When you imitate Jesus, you imitate God. If you struggle to understand the things of God, study the life of Christ. He will show you how to live. Jesus is the picture of a godly life. Match your life to His and you will show the world what it looks like to be a true Christ follower.

DAY 247

Jesus Loved the Poor

"The Spirit of the Lord is on me, because he has anointed me to preach good news to the poor. He has sent me to proclaim release to the captives and recovery of sight to the blind, to set free the oppressed." (Luke 4:18)

When was the last time you saw a homeless person on the cover of a teen magazine? Probably never. The world does not care for the poor or the broken. But that's exactly who Jesus loved. It's who He served and it's who He ministered to. The poor, the sick, and the lonely surrounded Jesus, thirsty for love and healing. When we draw close to God, we have eyes for the poor. We aren't repulsed by the hurting or the lonely. God wants to love the poor through you. He wants to use you to help the hurting. Who do you know who is poor, either physically or spiritually? Who could use a friend? Let God love them through you.

DAY 248

Jesus Humiliated Evil

He disarmed the rulers and authorities and disgraced
them publicly; he triumphed over them in him. (Colossians 2:15)

When Jesus rose from the dead, He didn't just barely beat Satan—He destroyed him. It wasn't a close fight. Jesus absolutely crushed Satan and defeated him forever. You can be confident that Christ in you does the same thing. He is able to totally destroy any sin that comes against you. In Christ, you can overcome every bad habit and every fear. Nothing is allowed to rule over you any more. The worst Satan can do to you is try to distract you from who you are in Christ. He cannot have your heart or your soul. That gives us so much confidence. Your God has already won the battle and defeated the enemy. Scripture said He not only beat him, He disgraced him. He took away all Satan's power and broke the chains from your life. The battle is over, and God won. You have the victory through Christ. Are you living it?

DAY 249

Jesus Spent Time Alone with God

He was praying in a certain place, and when he finished, one of his disciples said to him, "Lord, teach us to pray, just as John also taught his disciples." (Luke 11:1)

Very early in the morning, while it was still dark, he got up, went out, and made his way to a deserted place, and there he was praying. (Mark 1:35)

Have you ever been in the car with your parents when you almost ran out of gas? It's so stressful as you hurry to the nearest gas station. It doesn't matter how clean, new, or expensive the car is, if it doesn't have gas, it's totally useless. We're the same way in Christ. We have to have fuel to live the Christian life. That fuel comes from spending time alone with God. Even Jesus spent time alone with God. He went off to pray by Himself. It's hard to find that quiet time with God during the day. Tons of distractions fight for our attention. When you make time with God a priority, however, you have all the strength you need to face the day. The more time you spend with God, the more you look like Him. The more peace, joy, and patience you have. So fuel up in the presence of God every day. You'll have the energy you need to live for Him.

DAY 250

Jesus Healed the Sick

Jesus replied to them, "It is not those who are healthy who need a doctor, but those who are sick. I have not come to call the righteous, but sinners to repentance." (Luke 5:31–32)

Think about a time when you were really sick—high fever, trouble breathing, stomach virus, or all of that at one time. What if your mom took you to the hospital, and they told you, "I'm sorry, we can't see you. You're too sick." You would be very confused. When you're really sick, that's when you need a doctor. There's no such thing as being too sick for the hospital. It's the same with God. Jesus came to help people who are spiritually sick. A lot of times we think we're too bad to come to God, like we have to clean up our lives before we can pray to Him. The opposite is true. He is the one who heals us. We must go to Him when we're struggling with sin because He's the only one who can make us clean. There's no problem so bad that His presence can't fix. You're never too bad to come to God, and He will never turn you away.

Jesus Cried

Jesus wept. (John 11:35)

Girls often get teased for being so emotional, but did you know that Jesus also had strong emotions? He felt all the things you feel: anger, joy, excitement, and sorrow. More than once in Scripture, Jesus even cried. The Son of God was so overcome with emotion that He wept. Emotions are part of who we are as humans. As girls, we feel things deeply, and that's exactly how God made us to be. That doesn't mean your emotions can be an excuse for sinful behavior. Jesus never let His emotions drive Him to disobey God. So the next time you feel something strongly, take that emotion to God. Know that God understands your emotions because He gave them to you.

Jesus Did Miracles

Then he took the five loaves and the two fish, and looking up to heaven, he blessed and broke them. He kept giving them to the disciples to set before the crowd. Everyone ate and was filled. They picked up twelve baskets of leftover pieces. (Luke 9:16–17)

When Jesus walked on the earth, He performed many miracles. He fed thousands with a small meal; He healed the blind; He calmed a terrible storm. Every miracle accomplished a spiritual as well as a physical purpose. Jesus still works miracles today. He still heals people, and He still rescues. The most amazing miracles, however, happen in the hearts of His followers. God takes the heart of a lost person and totally transforms it. He takes our old desires and attitudes and gives us His desires and attitudes. In Christ, you are the biggest miracle you will ever see.

DAY 253

Jesus Searched for the Lost

"What man among you, who has a hundred sheep and loses one of them, does not leave the ninety-nine in the open field and go after the lost one until he finds it? . . . And coming home, he calls his friends and neighbors together, saying to them, 'Rejoice with me, because I have found my lost sheep!'" (Luke 15:4, 6)

Have you ever lost something really important, like your house key, cell phone, money, or purse? It's the worst feeling ever. You think you have it with you, and all of a sudden you realize you left it somewhere else. What do you do next? You look for it. You turn your house upside down. You pray a lot that no one stole it. For a few hours, nothing else matters but the thing you lost. That's exactly how Jesus is with us. He searches for us with all His heart. When we are far from God, He goes looking for us. He doesn't wait for us to come to Him. He loves you so much that He is passionate about bringing you back to Himself. He will not rest until you are His. When you finally find the thing you're looking for, you are so happy and relieved. It's the same with Christ. When you come to God, He is absolutely overjoyed and He celebrates over you. Know that your Savior loves you so much that He notices when you're far from Him, and He rushes to bring you back.

DAY 254

He Used Scripture to Fight Temptation

Then Jesus was led up by the Spirit into the wilderness to be tempted by the devil. . . . He answered, "It is written: Man must not live on bread alone but on every word that comes from the mouth of God." (Matthew 4:1, 4)

You can't use a baseball bat to kill a fly. When it comes to taking down your enemy, it's all about the weapon you choose. Jesus knew this. After He'd been fasting for weeks, Jesus went into the desert and was tempted by Satan. Temptation is when you feel the pull to do something you know is wrong. Rather than fighting with the weapon of His own strength or His own opinions, Jesus used Bible verses to destroy temptation. Each time Satan tempted Him to do something wrong, Jesus used the Bible as a sword to slice and dice the enemy's lies. We can use the Bible as a weapon against Satan too. To use this weapon, we have to know it. When you study God's Word, memorize it, journal about it, and talk about it, it stays on your heart. Then every time the enemy tries to tempt you, you can use a Bible verse to prove him wrong. What kind of sword are you using to fight against temptation? Pick up the sword of the Word of God and take your enemy down.

DAY 255

Jesus Washed the Disciples' Feet

Next, he poured water into a basin and began to wash his disciples' feet and to dry them with the towel tied around him. (John 13:5)

Imagine if the president of the United States knocked on your door one day holding a bucket and a mop, and he offered to clean your bathroom. You'd probably say something like, "No, Mr. President, you don't need to clean my bathroom." Instead, you would invite him to sit down as a guest. Cleaning bathrooms is not something presidents usually do.

Jesus was much more important than any US president, yet He did something more humiliating than clean bathrooms; He washed the feet of His disciples. One by one He put their dirty feet in a bowl and washed and dried them—something only a servant would have done. Jesus did this to teach us how we are supposed to serve the people around us. We're never supposed to think we're better than anyone else. We're to put ourselves last and always have eyes to see how we can serve the people around us. Whom can you serve today? What project can you do for someone that might seem too hard or too embarrassing? Jesus washed His friends' feet. We're supposed to do the same with how we serve our world.

Jesus Takes Away Our Stress

"My yoke is easy and my burden is light." (Matthew 11:30)

Sometimes a girl is just tired. Every day you juggle school, clubs, sports, church, chores, homework, and a whole bunch of other commitments. It's easy to feel overwhelmed. Does God just add to the list of things we're supposed to do? Not at all. Jesus tells us that His purpose is not to add stress to our already crowded lives. He teaches that His burden is light. In fact, He is a source of rest to us. When you feel overwhelmed, run to God. His number one goal for you is just that you would come sit in His presence. He wants to pour His love on you. He is the source of strength to do everything else on your list. If you're feeling tired or just busy, come to Christ. He will refresh you and remind you of the things that really matter in Him.

Jesus Ripped the Veil

Jesus let out a loud cry and breathed his last. Then the curtain of the temple was torn in two from top to bottom. (Mark 15:37–38)

Before Christ, people could die just by being in the presence of God. Once a year, a priest would purify himself through animal sacrifice and all kinds of other rituals. Then he had to go into the holiest part of the temple, and if he was clean enough, the presence of God would meet with him in this special room. This holy room was separated by a veil, so no one except the priest could enter. When Jesus died on the cross, the Bible says that veil was torn in two. That means that everyone can come to God through Christ. You don't have to make animal sacrifices for your sins because Jesus was your sacrifice. You don't have to go to the church or temple to meet with God because He lives inside you. His holiness stays in you as His follower. God loves you so much that He made the way to have a relationship with you. The veil separating your sin from His holiness is torn apart. You now have full access to God, your Father. Let that truth sink into your heart today. You are so loved by God, He ripped the veil for you.

DAY 258

Jesus Calmed the Storms

They came and woke him up, saying, "Master, Master, we're going to die!" Then he got up and rebuked the wind and the raging waves. So they ceased, and there was a calm. He said to them, "Where is your faith?" They were fearful and amazed, asking one another, "Who then is this? He commands even the winds and the waves, and they obey him!" (Luke 8:24–25)

It was the worst storm the disciples had probably ever seen. These were tough fishermen who spent their lives on the water—they weren't usually afraid of a little rough water. But this storm left them crying like kittens in a level 5 hurricane. And where was Jesus in this life-threatening storm? Sound asleep! No, He didn't take a Tylenol PM; He was just that peaceful. When the seas rage and the storm surges, the Son of God is not afraid. When we go through something hard, we can have this kind of peace. We don't have to be stressed or worried like the disciples. God is in control of your life, not money, friends, sickness, or your grades. When Jesus finally calmed the waves, He asked the disciples why they didn't have faith. The bigger miracle isn't calming the storm; it's the ability to sleep through it. Trust your Father and you can have peace right in the middle of every storm.

DAY 259

Gospel Rerun

Restore the joy of your salvation to me,
and sustain me by giving me a willing spirit. (Psalm 51:12)

On Christmas Day it never fails that several TV stations will play the same movie all day long. The first time you might actually watch the movie. But later in the day, it just plays in the background. You've already seen it so many times, that you don't really pay attention anymore. This can start to be how we respond to the gospel in our lives. We've heard the story of Christ so many times that it just starts to fade into the background of our lives. Don't let this happen. Ask God to make the story of Jesus stay alive in your hearts just like the first time you heard it. Think about what Christ did for you and let the beauty of it sink in. His love for you is real and beautiful. His story has power in our lives every single day.

DAY
260

Fix Our Eyes on Jesus

Keeping our eyes on Jesus, the source and perfecter
of our faith. For the joy that lay before him, he endured
the cross, despising the shame, and sat down
at the right hand of the throne of God. (Hebrews 12:2)

Have you ever ridden with an older sibling or a parent who got distracted while driving? It's pretty scary. You want to scream, "Stop texting or stop messing with the radio, and drive!" When you take your eyes off the road, you can't safely drive a car. It's the same in our relationship with God. We must focus our eyes on Christ in order to live for Him. So many things try to distract us: friends, boys, just being busy. But when we focus on Christ, those things don't have power over us. He is the source of our faith. He is the only one who has the answers and the help we need. If you're focusing on something else right now, stop and redirect your gaze to Jesus. He is the only one who can steer our lives the way He wants them to go.

DAY 261

Raised from the Dead

If Christ has not been raised, your faith is worthless;
you are still in your sins. (1 Corinthians 15:17)

When Christ rose from the dead, He defeated death forever. He took our sins on Himself and died on the cross, but that wasn't the end of the story. On the third day, the stone rolled away from the tomb and our Savior was alive. The Resurrection is so important to our lives as Christians. It's everything to our salvation. Jesus defeated death, meaning when we trust God as our Savior, we can live forever with Him in heaven. Sometimes we place so much emphasis on Jesus' death that we forget He's not still dead. Our Savior is alive now and forever, and He makes us alive as well. Let that truth sink into your heart and fill you with joy.

DAY 262

Tagline for Our Lives

I decided to know nothing among you except
Jesus Christ and him crucified. (1 Corinthians 2:2)

Most companies have quick mission statements, or tag lines, so you recognize their brand. It quickly tells you everything you need to know about their company. In Corinthians, Paul tells his mission statement as a follower of Christ: "Jesus Christ and Him crucified." The whole story of the gospel boils down to these five simple words. We were dead in sin, then Jesus died for us and rose from the dead. We now live a new life in Him. It's easy to get distracted by discussions of faith and how we're supposed to live. We need to be reminded of the simplicity of the gospel—it's all about Jesus and what He did for us. So the next time you need a reminder of what life's all about, remember Jesus Christ and Him crucified. And everything will come into focus again.

DAY 263

Jesus Is Coming Back

"Look, I am coming soon! Blessed is the one who keeps the words of the prophecy of this book." (Revelation 22:7)

Jesus is coming again. No one knows when or how it will happen, but He is coming back. As Christians, we get to look forward to Christ's coming as a day of great joy. It will be the most incredible, joyous day we could possibly imagine. Sometimes it's easy in the busyness of life to forget that our Savior will return to get us. In fact, the enemy wants us to forget about it. When we remember that Jesus is returning, we can face anything with joy. Little things that might make us upset suddenly don't matter any more. Look forward to Christ's return. God loves you so much and will come again for you.

Not a Bedtime Story

*For we did not follow cleverly contrived myths when we made
known to you the power and coming of our Lord Jesus Christ;
instead, we were eyewitnesses of his majesty. (2 Peter 1:16)*

At some point, all children believe that a make-believe story is real.
That's because kids have trouble telling the difference between truth
and fiction. As we get older, we realize which stories are real and which
ones are not. You never have to doubt God's Word as truth. Every story,
every person, and every promise is real. Peter reminds us that he was
an eyewitness to the resurrection of the Lord. He saw with his own eyes
that Jesus was brought back to life as the risen Son of God. He saw the
miracles of Jesus. Almost all the stories in the Bible were written by
people who saw them happen and had their lives changed. You can trust
the Word of God to be accurate in everything it tells you, and you can trust
it to be the perfect guide for your life.

DAY 265

Who Was Jesus?

*"But you," he asked them, "who do you say that I am?" Simon
Peter answered, "You are the Messiah, the Son of the living God!"
(Matthew 16:15–16)*

The world has a lot of ideas about who Jesus is. Some say He was a
great prophet who spoke the deep things of God. Some say Jesus was a
good teacher who told good stories and taught us how to live. Some say
He was a good person who loved the poor and healed the sick. Jesus is
much more than all of this. He is the Son of God. Although Jesus was a
man, He was fully God as well. God became a man and walked around
with us so we could know Him and have a relationship with Him. Never
let other people confuse you about the true identity of Christ. The world
will call Him a teacher and a prophet, but they will not call Him God. You
know better. Jesus is none other than the Savior of the world, the Son of
God, and the one who will come again as King of kings and Lord of lords.

DAY 266

The Day Is Unknown, the Plan Is Sure

"Now concerning that day or hour no one knows—neither the angels in heaven nor the Son—but only the Father." (Mark 13:32)

A lot of people try to predict when Jesus will return. Some read the Bible for clues and point to a certain date. Any time someone has tried to give a date and time for Christ's return, that time has come and gone, and the person looks silly. That's because nobody can predict Jesus' Second Coming. The Bible says not even the angels know. It will happen without warning or man's predictions. Don't spend time trying to figure out when it will happen. Spend your energy getting close to God, living for Him, and spreading the gospel. When it will happen doesn't matter because it will happen. Our Savior will come again for us, and it will be a joyful day. Get ready for Him and look forward to His coming, but don't worry about figuring out the exact moment of His coming.

No Other Way

"Don't let you heart be troubled. Believe in God; believe also in me." . . . Jesus told him, "I am the way, the truth, and the life. No one comes to the Father except through me." (John 14:1, 6)

There is salvation in no one else, for there is no other name under heaven given to people by which we must be saved. (Acts 4:12)

Have you ever had to go a different way to school because of traffic or construction? It's annoying and it might take longer, but it still gets you there. This is not how it works with God. There is only one path to God and that is through His Son, Jesus Christ. There aren't any alternates or detours you can take. All the religions of the world do not lead to God. Jesus Himself teaches that no one comes to God except through Him. There is no other name given to people for salvation except the name of Jesus. Don't be fooled. It's popular to claim that all religions are just different roads that lead to the same God. It's popular to say that Buddha, Mohammad, and Jesus are just different names for the same God. This is a lie. Other gods are false and do not offer salvation. Jesus alone offers salvation and an everlasting relationship with God. Put your faith in Him and He will lead you to God and to an eternity in heaven.

DAY 268

Real Life

"A thief comes only to steal and kill and destroy. I have come so that they may have life and have it in abundance." (John 10:10)

When we think of thieves, we think of shady guys dressed all in black, wearing masks and sneaking around. The enemy, Satan, isn't that kind of thief. He steals by holding out things you actually want—popularity, beauty, love—and he tempts you to get those things apart from Christ. He steals your joy, your peace, and your confidence. Girls, Jesus came so that you could have life. He came so you could be full of peace, full of confidence, full of hope. He is all about your complete joy. His rules are for our freedom. He came so you could have salvation, not so that you could walk around with a frown, while everyone else is having fun. Run after Him with all your heart, and don't look back. He will satisfy your heart and give you everything you need to live life to the fullest.

Worship

When you worship God, you adore Him with your heart and praise Him with your life. This section focuses on different ways and places to worship God.

DAY
269

Before You Worship

"So if you are offering your gift on the altar, and there you remember that your brother or sister has something against you, leave your gift there in front of the altar. First go and be reconciled with your brother or sister, and then come and offer your gift." (Matthew 5:23–24)

God doesn't just wish you'd get along with your friends, He demands it. When you fight with your sister in Christ, you cannot worship God with a clean heart. Fighting with others creates a giant barrier between you and God. The Bible tells us to go deal with the conflict. Settle your differences and make peace. He is glorified when you get along with each other. This is an act of worship before Him. Forgive and be forgiven so you can once again worship God. When you have unity with your fellow Christians, you can worship God together with nothing standing between you and God.

DAY 270

All Colors, All Languages, All People

The nations will bow in worship to [God]. (Zephaniah 2:11)

Sometimes it's easy to think that all Christians are from America, speak English, and are the same color. This couldn't be further from the truth—even Jesus didn't speak English. There are Christians all over the world from every tribe and every color who worship the same God you worship. One day, all the Christians around the world will stand before God and worship Him. The languages will be different, but the message will be the same. God loves all races and all peoples. He has a heart for the nations. The closer you get to God, the more you develop a heart for people of every color and language as well. One day thousands of men, women, and children of every color will praise God with all their hearts. We will join in this crowd as part of the very diverse body of Christ.

DAY 271

Out Loud, by Yourself

Our Lord and God, you are worthy to receive glory and honor and power, because you have created all things, and by your will they exist and were created. (Revelation 4:11)

We can worship God anytime and anywhere. You've probably attended a worship service at church and sung worship songs together. Have you ever practiced worshipping God by yourself? Try singing to Him in your room, outside, when you're alone in the house, or even in the shower! When you worship God by yourself, it is powerful, and He hears every word you sing. Worshipping God helps you silence the distractions of technology, friends, and the worries in your life. It reminds you that you are His daughter and He is your Father. He is worthy to receive glory and honor, so no matter what your voice sounds like, praise God with your whole heart.

DAY 272

Worship in Your Desk at School

Therefore, since we are receiving a kingdom that cannot be shaken, let us be thankful. By it, we may serve God acceptably, with reverence and awe. (Hebrews 12:28)

You can't really belt out a song in the middle of school, but you can still absolutely praise God in the classroom. In your mind, tell God how awesome He is. Tell Him why you love Him, and thank Him for all He's done for you that day. This kind of worship is a great way to focus your attention on God in the middle of your day. You can even write a letter to God or read your Bible. It doesn't need to take long. Just a few words of worship are enough to focus your heart back to God. He so loves to hear from you, and He cherishes every word you speak to Him. You are precious to Him, and He longs to be part of your whole day. Worship Him today.

DAY 273

Worship with Friends at Church

Enter his gates with thanksgiving and his courts with praise. Give thanks to him and bless his name. (Psalm 100:4)

It's sometimes easy to get distracted at church, especially when you're surrounded by friends. The next time you're in a worship service, try to really focus on your Savior. Think about the words you're singing on the screen or in the hymnal. Let the words reach your heart. Most likely your friends will follow your example and begin to focus too. There's something cool about being able to worship God beside your friends. It definitely draws you close together and reminds you of how much God loves you. Being part of a church is crucial for your spiritual growth. When you have an army of Christian friends and family at your side, you can face anything. So next time you're at church, commit to focus on God and praise His name with your whole heart. You will definitely get a huge blessing from worshipping with your friends and church family.

DAY 274

Worship Through Praise

Enter his gates with thanksgiving and his courts with praise.
Give thanks to him and bless his name. (Psalm 100:4)

When your mom goes through the drive-through to order fast food, and the server asks what you want, do you ever respond by saying, "I don't need anything. I just wanted to see how your day was going. Just wanted to tell you great job for all those burgers you've made today!" Never. You tell the server exactly what you want, and you expect to get it fast.

Some of us go to God with a list just like this. We come to Him with a list of what we want, but we don't stop to thank Him for who He is or what He's already done in our lives. Scripture tells us to enter His gates with praise and thanksgiving. The next time you pray, start by telling God how great He is. Thank Him for the cross, for your family, for anything you are thankful for. After focusing on how awesome God is, your list of demands might not be so long after all.

DAY 275

The Posture of Worship

Come, let us worship and bow down;
*let us kneel before the L*ORD *our Maker. (Psalm 95:6)*

The Bible is filled with all kinds of different examples of worship and all different kinds of worshippers. I think that's because no matter how we're feeling or where we are, worship can always be part of our lives. One way to worship God is by practicing a posture of worship. It's fine to stand and sing to God, but there are many other ways to worship as well that can reflect what we're feeling about the Lord. Bowing down before the Lord makes Him seem huge in our lives. It reminds us that He is King and bigger than all our problems. When we raise our hands, we declare that we surrender to God and declare that He is mighty. You may choose to sit, stand, kneel, or raise your hands. However you worship God, He hears your heart as well as your words and He loves it when you worship Him.

DAY 276

Worship in Nature

The heavens declare the glory of God, and the expanse proclaims the work of his hands. (Psalm 19:1)

Have you ever been in awe of the beauty of nature? Whether it was a sunset, a waterfall, a view of the mountains, or a clear starry night—God's hands made it all. Nature moves us to worship God. The beauty of creation makes us celebrate the Creator. Nature also reminds us how precious we are to God. His hands formed the universe, the sky, the sun, and the oceans. He paints the sunsets and lifts the mountains. Yet those very same hands also made you. The next time you see something in nature that catches your attention, even something as small as a flower, praise God. Remember how much He loves you and how beautifully you are made.

**DAY
277**

Worship When You're Feeling Thirsty

*As a deer longs for flowing streams,
so I long for you, God. I thirst for God, the living God.
When can I come and appear before God? (Psalm 42:1–2)*

Have you ever been so thirsty you would kill for a drink? On a hot summer's day playing outside or after a long sport's practice, you get that intense dry-mouthed, dizzy, exhausted kind of thirst. All you can think about is ice cold water. Did you know our souls crave water also? Not water in a cup, but the all-satisfying water of the presence of God. When you spend time in God's presence through prayer and worship, you nourish your soul. The more time you spend away from God, the more dehydrated and thirsty your soul gets. You can try to fill your soul with things the world offers like popularity, material possessions, or a beautiful image, but it just leaves your soul feeling cracked and dry. The only water that satisfies is Jesus. And the only way to find it is to know Him. Drink as much as you want whenever you need it. He is the only one able to quench your spiritual thirst.

DAY 278

Worship in an Ordinary Day

Better a day in your courts than a thousand anywhere else.
I would rather stand at the threshold of the house of my God
than to live in the tents of wicked people. (Psalm 84:10)

Do you have any idea how many blessings God longs to pour on your life? The presence of God is more joyful and more satisfying than anything the world tries to give you. He longs to give you His peace, His protection, and His wisdom. He knows the struggles you face and the temptation not to trust Him. What things try to distract you from His presence? Ignore them. Rather than having another ordinary day, dare to live each moment in the "courts" of the Lord. That means you live your day trusting God is right beside you, guiding you, loving you, and forgiving you. One day spent with Him is better than a thousand days trying to do things your way, in your own strength. Live today with Him, and enjoy all the blessings of walking with God.

Spiritual Act of Worship

*Therefore, brothers and sisters, in view of the mercies of God,
I urge you to present your bodies as a living sacrifice, holy and
pleasing to God; this is your true worship. (Romans 12:1)*

When you think of worship, you probably think of people at church singing songs. This is definitely worship, but did you know that actually worship is everything we do for God? The Bible tells us that more than songs, God desires us to "present [our] bodies" as worship. That means that everything we do, everything we think, and everything we speak can be used in worship to God. Were you kind to someone who didn't deserve it? That is worship. Did you obey your parents when they told you to do something? Worship. Worshipping God is about more than singing songs to Him. It's about pleasing Him in everything we do in the day. Of course, we mess up, but when we ask for forgiveness, that is also worship. What acts of worship will you do for God today?

DAY 280

Worship in the Morning

But I will sing of your strength and will joyfully proclaim
your faithful love in the morning. For you have been a stronghold
for me, a refuge in my day of trouble. (Psalm 59:16)

Bad breath. Frizzy hair. Screaming alarm clock. Hurrying to get ready. Mornings usually aren't much fun. That's probably why God's Word tells us to praise Him in the morning. God knows our mornings are the very start to our day. When you have a bad morning, it usually makes the whole day bad. But a good morning gets the whole day started off right. Even if you don't feel like it, try praising God in the mornings. You don't have to burst into song like a fairy princess singing to birds, but just pray quietly as you're getting ready. As you brush your hair, praise God for loving you so much that He knows how many hairs you have. When you get dressed, praise Him for clothing you with protection and love all day long. When you're in the car, ask to listen to worship music. A few little acts of worship like this will blast away the morning blues and bring a beautiful start to your day.

Joy

God wants you to have joy. Joy is a fruit of the Spirit found in Christ that makes us happy to obey God. When you're happy following God, you don't want to follow anything else. This section talks about how to find that joy and how it changes our lives.

DAY 281

No Other Good Thing

I said to the Lord, "You are my Lord;
I have nothing good besides You." (Psalm 16:2)

It's a bold thing to say, "I have nothing good except for God." That doesn't mean that you don't have any blessings. It means that you love God so much that without Him, you would be miserable. God is the source of all your blessings, and He gives meaning to every good thing in your life. Seek to love God so much that every other blessing in your life is second to Him. He delights to bless you, but He never wants those blessings to become your god. When God captures your heart, you cannot love anything as much as Him. Praise God for your blessings like family, friends, money, and health, but worship God and love Him with your whole heart.

DAY 282

Joy in Your Presence

You give him blessings forever;
you cheer him with joy in your presence. (Psalm 21:6)

Who is your funniest friend? A funny friend has your sense of humor and can make you laugh harder than anyone else. She can make you laugh any time of the day—even when you're supposed to be quiet. When the two of you get together, you might drive everyone else crazy, but you're totally happy laughing away. Just being around her puts you in a better mood. God wants to do the same thing for you. When you spend time in His presence, He will cheer you up. He knows how to lighten your problems and remind you of your blessings. He wants to give you joy you can't find anywhere else in the world. Not everything about God has to be serious all the time—sometimes He just wants to share in a silly moment with you. Invite Him into every part of your day and He will give you His joy.

DAY 283

Taste and See

Taste and see that the L<small>ORD</small> is good. How happy is the person who takes refuge in him! (Psalm 34:8)

This verse is awesome because it tells us to see the goodness of God for ourselves. We don't have to just rely on what our parents or our Sunday school teacher says about God. We can experience it for ourselves. Obviously we can't exactly see and taste God physically, but we can experience His presence and enjoy the blessings He gives us. The verse also promises us, "Happy is the man who takes refuge in him." When we follow God and experience His blessings, we are actually happy people. We don't have to be gloomy or depressed. His presence makes us joyful. It puts a smile on our face and kind words in our mouth. Today look for ways to taste and see the Lord is good. He will fill you with His happiness and joy.

DAY
284

Joy Is Powerful

*Restore the joy of your salvation to me,
and sustain me by giving me a willing spirit. (Psalm 51:12)*

We think of joy as the feeling we get on Christmas morning. It's taking a family vacation to the beach and watching a sunset. But true joy found in Christ is a whole lot more powerful than a warm feeling. Joy in Christ is the most powerful weapon you have against the enemy. Joy means you are totally satisfied and fulfilled in God alone. Joy in Christ means that everything else in your life—friends, family, stuff, popularity, clothes, your own wishes—pales in comparison to knowing God. When you are truly happy in Him, that joy overshadows all other desires. Right now, God offers you the pure, lasting, all-satisfying joy of His presence. Choose to live in that joy.

DAY 285

Good to Be Near God

*But as for me, God's presence is my good. I have made the
Lord God my refuge, so I can tell about all you do. (Psalm 73:28)*

When your mean teacher says, "I need to see you at my desk after school," it's usually not a good thing. You feel a kind of sick dread for the rest of the day, wondering, *What did I do now?!* God is nothing like this. While being in the presence of your mean teacher is horrible, being in the presence of God is good! He longs for you to come close to Him, not so He can accuse you of sin or whack you with a holy ruler. He loves you, and He wants to bless you. He wants to be your refuge, your healer, your encouragement, and your safe place. He wants to share your life—your happiest moments and your saddest. You can call to God any time of day from any place. He loves to be near to you. So change your perspective and start spending time in the presence of God. He loves you so much.

Leadership

The world needs godly girls to step up and lead. This section deals with how girls of all personalities can become leaders in their schools, homes, and churches.

DAY
286

The First Act of a Leader

Let us watch out for one another to provoke love and good works.
(Hebrews 10:24)

The world is desperate for leadership. Whether you're quiet and thoughtful, or loud and energetic, you have the makings of a leader. To become a godly leader, the first thing you have to do is get the attention off yourself. Good leaders focus on the people around them and serve them. Leaders know how to encourage and motivate other people to take action by showing them how it's done. Everyone has someone following them. Whether it's a group of friends or your younger brothers and sisters, someone needs your leadership in their life. As you follow God, people will follow you. Lead with courage and set the example of how to be a godly girl. Who knows what God will accomplish through you.

DAY 287

The Quiet Leader

What is inside the heart—the imperishable quality of a gentle and quiet spirit, which is of great worth in God's sight. (1 Peter 3:4)

She's loud, she's popular, and everyone wants to be around her. She's the typical picture of a leader. We usually think of leaders as being loud and bossy. They have an easy time telling other people what to do, and people generally follow. But there's another kind of leader—a quiet leader. Just because you don't have a loud personality doesn't mean you can't lead people for Christ. In fact, guess who usually likes a quiet leader? Quiet people. If you're a quiet, determined, behind-the-scenes girl, your friends are probably like that too. You can influence the people around you just by being yourself. Just because you don't lead with a parade marching behind you doesn't mean you can't lead. The world needs quiet leaders who serve out of the spotlight. Your friends need to see someone step up and do the right thing even when it's hard. So embrace your God-given personality and lead exactly how God has made you to lead.

DAY 288

Following the (Wrong) Leader

The leaders of the people mislead them,
and those they mislead are swallowed up. (Isaiah 9:16)

"Be on your guard against false prophets who come to you
in sheep's clothing but inwardly are ravaging wolves.
You'll recognize them by their fruit. Are grapes gathered from
thornbushes or figs from thistles?" (Matthew 7:15–16)

Did you know there are hundreds of older girls lining up to be your role models? They call out to you from your favorite TV shows, your favorite music and magazines. They say, "Follow me, and I'll teach you how to dress cute, be popular, talk to guys, and be cool." The Bible says to choose carefully whom you follow. No girl can force herself to be your role model. You have the power to choose whom you follow. Before you imitate someone, look at her life. Does she love God? Is she kind? Scripture says you can tell the truth about someone by the fruit in their lives. A girl can be beautiful, successful, and popular and totally go against God with her actions. Choose mentors who will push you closer to Christ. Don't allow any girl to influence you who isn't dedicated to knowing God and living for Him. You get to choose whom you follow. Choose wisely because she will have a powerful influence on your life.

DAY 289

Leading at Church

*Don't let anyone despise your youth, but set
an example for the believers in speech, in conduct,
in love, in faith, and in purity. (1 Timothy 4:12)*

Pastors, deacons, Sunday school teachers—there are plenty of people at your church who are older and more experienced than you. But did you know your church still needs your leadership? You have influence and power at your church to set an example and encourage others in their faith. Scripture even tells you to set an example for older believers. You can lead at church in several ways: by worshipping God with your whole heart, by serving and teaching those younger than you, by tithing money you make from your allowance or job, by being respectful to those older than you, by sharing the gospel with your friends. Just because you're young doesn't mean you can't lead. In fact, sometimes it takes the faith of a young girl to inspire and encourage those who are older in Christ. How are you leading at church? Your church needs you to step out and reflect Christ.

DAY 290

When Nobody Follows

*You supported me because of my integrity
and set me in your presence forever. (Psalm 41:12)*

Sometimes when you make a hard decision, you have to make it alone. It's so tough when you do the right thing and realize none of your friends are behind you. Trust God. He sees your integrity and your good character. He knows your heart and your commitment to His commands. Be encouraged that your example and your stand for Him do not go unnoticed. Who knows, but the next time one of your friends may remember your example and do the right thing. It's painful to stand for God when you're by yourself, but it is much more painful to walk away from God and do the wrong thing. Remember, even when your friends walk away, God will never abandon you. He is with you always.

DAY 291

Girl After God's Own Heart

*But now your kingdom will not endure; the L<small>ORD</small> has sought out
a man after his own heart and appointed him ruler of his people,
because you have not kept the L<small>ORD</small>'s command. (1 Samuel 13:14 NIV)*

King David was one of the greatest leaders in the Bible. Long before he was king of a nation, he honored God in the small daily tasks of his life. When he became king, he ruled with integrity and wisdom. When he made mistakes, he turned to God for forgiveness. He was described as a "man after [God's] own heart." David's strength in leading came because he loved God. God wants to accomplish great things in your life. He wants to use you to spread His love and His gospel to other people. To be a great leader for God, you don't need incredible earthly strength or intelligence. You just need to love God with your whole heart. As you become a girl after God's heart, you will be a leader for His name.

DAY 292

For Such a Time as This

If you keep silent at this time, relief and deliverance will come to the Jewish people from another place, but you and your father's family will be destroyed. Who knows, perhaps you have come to your royal position for such a time as this. (Esther 4:14)

Sometimes we don't ask to be the leader, but we become one anyway. Esther was an ordinary Jewish girl, chosen to marry the king of Persia. She eventually kept her entire nation from being destroyed. She was in the right place at the right time to make a difference. You are also in the right place at the right time to influence people for God. God has placed you in your family, school, church, and community to lead others to know Him more. Ask God to give you courage to live your faith every day. You don't have to have all the answers, just a heart for God. He will work through you when you step out in faith. He has brought you exactly where you are for such a time as this.

Just Give

A sign of being with Jesus is the desire to give. This section deals with the power of giving to people in need.

DAY 293

Give to the Poor

Staring at him in awe, he said, "What is it, Lord?"
The angel told him, "Your prayers and your acts of charity have
ascended as a memorial offering before God." (Acts 10:4)

What if you suddenly had to survive with only one pair of shoes? That's actually how most of the world lives now. Most girls don't have closets full of clothes and shoe racks full of shoes or a jewelry box full of accessories. Even if you don't think of yourself as rich, trust me, in the world's eyes, you are rich. There are girls just like you in real physical need—maybe even in your class at school. Pray about what you can do to help someone in need physically. You can donate clothes to a clothing drive. You can give food to a food bank. You can buy extra school supplies for a girl who can't afford it. You don't have to look far to find someone in need. Ask God to open your eyes to the needs around you and ask Him to show you who you and your family might be able to help.

DAY
294

Give Your Friendship

*A friend loves at all times, and a brother is born
for a difficult time. (Proverbs 17:17)*

You know that girl. She sits by herself at lunch; she wears funny clothes. She might have a physical disability or a social one. No one really wants to be around her. You might feel sorry for her, but what she really needs is a friend. She needs the protection and joy from knowing she's not alone. You can be her friend. I know there are few things as scary and risky as being the friend of a girl no one likes, but God will be with you. He knows the courage it takes to be friends with someone who's different. Take another friend along with you and make friends with her. She will be so happy, but more than that, your heavenly Father will be greatly pleased with you. He was friends with the outcasts too.

DAY 295

Give Godly Advice

Without guidance, a people will fall, but with many counselors there is deliverance. (Proverbs 11:14)

Every girl hears this question from a friend: "What should I do?" The next time one of your friends asks you for advice, think about your answer. Instead of giving her advice from your own ideas, give her advice from God's Word. Find Bible verses that deal with her problem and offer spiritual guidance. If it's something the Bible doesn't specifically talk about, then pray with her about the issue. God's opinion is so much more valuable than your own advice. Be the kind of friend who points your friends to God in every situation. His advice will always come through for her.

DAY 296

Give Forgiveness

Therefore, as God's chosen ones, holy and dearly loved,
put on compassion, kindness, humility, gentleness, and patience,
bearing with one another and forgiving one another if anyone
has a grievance against another. Just as the Lord has
forgiven you, so you are also to forgive. (Colossians 3:12–13)

When a friend lets us down, we have a decision to make. We can end the friendship or we can forgive. If we end a friendship every time we have a fight, we're going to have some pretty short friendships. As followers of Christ, we need to be quick to forgive. When we remember how much God has forgiven us, it becomes easy to forgive someone else. Forgiveness isn't easy, and it doesn't mean you always trust someone again immediately. It just means that the person doesn't owe you anything. You trust God, not yourself, to bring justice. So the next time your friend messes up, forgive her. Before too long, you'll probably need that same forgiveness from her in return.

DAY 297

Don't Be a Sponge

"Give to the one who asks you, and don't turn away from the one who wants to borrow from you." (Matthew 5:42)

Have you ever smelled a dirty sponge? It's pretty gross. A sponge gets dirty when it absorbs a bunch of water and then just sits there. As time passes, that water molds and stinks. That's because sponges were designed to wring out water, not hold it in. The same thing can happen to us as Christians. When we hear about God, read the Bible, and sing worship songs, but don't actually live out what we learn, we get spiritually stinky. When we soak in the things of God, but don't let it change our behavior, how we talk to our parents, how we treat our friends, how we treat our siblings, we start to smell bad. So as you read your Bible and go to church, remember to live out what you learn. Use what you learn to help you live a changed life for Christ and you will smell sweet.

DAY 298

Give Love

The commandments, Do not commit adultery; do not murder; do not steal; do not covet; and any other commandment, are summed up by this commandment: Love your neighbor as yourself. (Romans 13:9)

Let's be honest, sometimes the only person who doesn't get on your nerves is the girl starring back at you from the mirror. We love ourselves. We get most of our attention and care. We feed ourselves every day. We take a shower and get ourselves dressed. We look out for ourselves. We don't let ourselves walk into traffic or juggle knives. The Bible says that we're supposed to love other people just like this. It's not that we're supposed to feed other people or get them dressed, but we take care of others. We give them attention just like we give ourselves attention. We listen to them and help meet their needs. In fact, you can tell how much a girl loves God by how much she loves other people. So glance up from the mirror and put your eyes on the people around you—your friends, your neighbors, your family. When you love other people, you want to bring them good, not harm. You will love and serve them as much as you love and serve yourself. God will be glorified through that love.

Salvation

Jesus died on the cross and defeated the grave, and His salvation covers our sins. In Him, we are made new. This sections walks through the steps of salvation, baptism, and the transforming work of God in our lives.

DAY 299

Born This Way

Indeed, I was guilty when I was born;
I was sinful when my mother conceived me. (Psalm 51:5)

There's a lie that says whoever you are and whatever you struggle with is okay because you were "born this way." This is far from the truth. God's Word says we were born into sin, separated from His presence. We were born with sinful desires and the need to serve ourselves. Even the best person you can think of was born into sin. Sin isn't what we do; it's who we are. We all need a Savior. That's why Jesus came. He came to pay for our sins on the cross. He loves us so much, He would never leave us in our sin. He rescues us and is forever transforming us to look more like Him. So the next time someone excuses their behavior by saying, "I was born this way," just remember that we were all born into sin. And we all need a Savior.

DAY 300

Come to Christ

If you confess with your mouth, "Jesus is Lord," and believe in your heart that God raised him from the dead, you will be saved. One believes with the heart, resulting in righteousness, and one confesses with the mouth, resulting in salvation. (Romans 10:9–10)

The Bible tells us exactly how to have salvation through Christ. It is by His work on the cross we are saved. He died and rose again, paying for our sins. That sacrifice applied to our lives is all we need to come to God. The Bible says when you confess with your mouth and believe in your heart, you will be saved. That doesn't mean these are magic words. When you come to Christ for salvation, you're saying you want to follow the way of Christ. You want to trade His life for your life, His desires for your desires, and His actions for your actions. You don't have to be good enough to come to God. He takes you exactly as you are. You also don't have to know lots of the Bible. God wants a relationship with you, and that is only possible in Christ. If you have never decided to follow Christ for salvation, talk to your parents. It is the most amazing, life-changing decision you will ever make.

DAY
301

His Work, Not Yours

For you are saved by grace through faith,
and this is not from yourselves; it is God's gift—
not from works, so that no one can boast. (Ephesians 2:8–9)

How do you make an A on your report card? You study, you work hard, and you pay attention in class. The harder you work, the more likely you will do well on a test. This strategy works in the classroom, but it is not how God works. You can't do any work to earn God's love. No amount of good works will make God love you more or get you close to salvation. The only way to have a relationship with God is through faith in Jesus. A lifetime of good works cannot come close to matching the holiness of God. That's why Jesus did the work of salvation for you. He died on the cross and rose from the grave. Come to Christ just as you are. Then He saves you and begins to do good works in your life.

DAY 302

I'm Not Sure I'm Saved

Therefore, he is able to save completely those who come to God through him, since he always lives to intercede for them. (Hebrews 7:25)

Have you ever wondered if you were really saved? It would be nice if everyone who was saved suddenly looked different on the outside, but that doesn't happen. If you have truly given your life to God through Jesus, then you are saved. There is nothing that can take away your salvation. The Holy Spirit is sealed forever in your life, and you are a daughter of God. Remember, you didn't do anything to earn your own salvation, so you can't do anything to lose it either. If you need assurance, trust God's Word that says, "He is able to save completely those who come to God through him." Seek God and love Him with your whole heart. The closer you get to God, the more you will feel the confidence of your salvation. Your Savior loves you, and He paid the price for your sins. He holds you in His arms now and forever.

Baptism

*Peter replied, "Repent and be baptized, each of you,
in the name of Jesus Christ for the forgiveness of your sins,
and you will receive the gift of the Holy Spirit." (Acts 2:38)*

If you've ever played a sport, you've probably gotten to wear a uniform. Your jersey or uniform signals to everyone who sees you that you are part of that team. When you take the jersey off after a game, (hopefully to wash it), you're still on the team. Like your uniform represents your team, baptism represents salvation. When you're baptized, you tell the world that you have been saved and you are part of the family of God. Baptism doesn't save you. There's nothing magical about the water. Only Christ can give salvation. But God wants you to follow salvation with baptism because you're telling the world what God has done in your life. Your baptism and your story of salvation also encourages other people to come to God.

DAY 304

You Can't Change Yourself

Are you so foolish? After beginning with the Spirit, are you now finishing by the flesh? (Galatians 3:3)

When we came to Christ for salvation, He did all the work. We couldn't be good enough or smart enough to erase our own sins. We gladly accept Christ's work on the cross as a substitute for our sins. But a funny thing happens after salvation. We think it's up to us to become holy. The power that saved you is the same power that changes you. It's not up to you to be good on your own after coming to Christ. His Spirit lives inside you and will continue to change you. What do you have to do? Stay close to God. Run after Him and seek Him with your whole heart. Spend time in His presence and worship Him. Then He will change you through His work, not your own. He doesn't save you and then leave you to fix yourself. He does all the work. All you have to do is stay close to Him and allow Him to change you.

The Fruit of the Spirit

The fruit of the Spirit is everything we get when God saves us through Christ. The closer we are to Him, the more that fruit is displayed in our lives. This section helps us understand the fruit of the Spirit and how to enjoy it by staying in the presence of God.

DAY
305

The Fruit of the Spirit

For the fruit of the light consists of all goodness, righteousness, and truth. (Ephesians 5:9)

When you come to Christ, the Bible says you're a new creation. That doesn't mean you grow wings or morph into some weird new creature. It means that a radical transformation happens on the inside, in your heart. You have new desires and new loves. You have the freedom to seek God and come to Him whenever you want. Best of all, you have the fruit of the Spirit. The fruit of the Spirit is the evidence of a saved life. It's everything good God gives you when you come to Him. You can't produce it on your own, and you can't fake it. It is real and genuine and only found in the lives of Christ followers. The fruit of the Spirit is love, joy, peace, patience, kindness, goodness, faithfulness, gentleness, and self-control. It's everything Christ demonstrated while He was on the earth, and it's everything we get to have when we come to Him.

DAY 306

Love

But the fruit of the Spirit is love, joy, peace, patience, kindness, goodness, faithfulness. . . . Now those who belong to Christ Jesus have crucified the flesh with its passions and desires. (Galatians 5:22, 24)

The world has a messed-up definition of love. Movies tell us that love is a fuzzy feeling in our hearts, a burning fire when two people like each other. The world tells us that we can fall in and out of love as our feelings change. In Christ, the fruit of love is so much stronger and more powerful than the world's. In fact, only Christians know what real love is. When we come to God, we have the power to really love other people. We can love in a way that's totally selfless. We can love with actions and deeds and not just words and feelings. We even have the power to love our enemies, something the world will never do. How have you seen the fruit of love in your life since becoming a Christian? Real love is something the world is desperate to see. You can show it to them because you have the fruit of the Spirit in your life.

DAY 307

Joy

But the fruit of the Spirit is love, joy, peace, patience, kindness, goodness, faithfulness. . . . Now those who belong to Christ Jesus have crucified the flesh with its passions and desires. (Galatians 5:22, 24)

Have you ever watched your parents try to strike a match in the wind? It lights up for a second, then quickly blows out. That's exactly like the happiness of the world. The world finds something that makes them happy, but it only lasts for a short time and then it goes away. Then they need something else to make them happy. In Christ, we have the fruit of the Spirit—joy. Joy is like happiness, except it lasts forever. It shines like the Olympic torch, which burns even in pouring rain. Joy doesn't depend on your circumstance or your situation. If you know Christ, you have the fruit of joy in your life. You can have it whenever you need it because it comes straight from God. Practice having joy today. The world will notice and wonder why you're different.

DAY 308

Peace

But the fruit of the Spirit is love, joy, peace, patience, kindness, goodness, faithfulness. . . . Now those who belong to Christ Jesus have crucified the flesh with its passions and desires. (Galatians 5:22, 24)

Think about the most peaceful place you've ever seen. Maybe it's a beautiful ocean or a lake in nature. Maybe it's a majestic view of the mountains. You might not be able to sit in nature every day, but in Christ, you have that kind of peace inside you all the time. Even in the middle of a stressful day, rushing around, dealing with problems, you can access the peace of God. Peace is a fruit of the Spirit, which means everyone who comes to Christ gets it. His peace is able to protect you and keep you from worrying. The peace of Christ can guard your mind from stressful thoughts. His peace even impacts our relationships, helping you forgive. How have you seen the peace of Christ affect your life? The peace of God is His presence in our lives, helping us endure every situation that comes our way.

DAY 309

Patience

But the fruit of the Spirit is love, joy, peace, patience, kindness, goodness, faithfulness. . . . Now those who belong to Christ Jesus have crucified the flesh with its passions and desires. (Galatians 5:22, 24)

Nobody likes to wait. Our whole world is geared toward getting us what we want exactly when we want it. Everything from ordering food, shopping for clothes, and using technology to visiting amusement parks is designed to cut out the wait. There's nothing wrong with getting things fast except that it trains us to be impatient. Patience is a fruit of the Spirit that gives us the ability to wait without getting angry or worried. Patience helps us not fly off the handle when something or someone is running late. It also helps us trust God in the big things, when we can't see the answer to our prayers. The world has no concept of patience, but in Christ we have this gift. The closer we are to God, the more we show patience in our lives. While the world is constantly stressed, patience is a refreshing gift for your soul, found only in Christ. At some point today, you will have to wait for something. Instead of getting upset, practice the gift of patience that God has given you.

Kindness

But the fruit of the Spirit is love, joy, peace, patience, kindness, goodness, faithfulness. . . . Now those who belong to Christ Jesus have crucified the flesh with its passions and desires. (Galatians 5:22, 24)

Have you ever been forced to do something nice for your sibling? Maybe you were fighting and your mom made you clean each other's rooms. You're technically doing a good action, but you're not nice about it and you hate doing it. Kindness is doing the right thing with a truly great attitude. When you show kindness, you take joy in helping others. Even if the job itself isn't really fun, you can still have the attitude of Christ. Kindness is something the world is desperate for. The world doesn't understand why anyone would help someone else when they're not getting anything in return. If you know Christ, you have the fruit of kindness right now. You just have to practice it.

DAY 311

Goodness

But the fruit of the Spirit is love, joy, peace, patience, kindness, goodness, faithfulness. . . . Now those who belong to Christ Jesus have crucified the flesh with its passions and desires. (Galatians 5:22, 24)

Have you ever trash-talked someone? Trash talk happens before a sports game or board game. It's when you tell your opponent how good you are and how you're about to destroy them in the game. But when you sit down or take the field to play, trash talk no longer matters. It's all about who is more skilled and better prepared to win. The fruit of the Spirit—goodness—is like that. Anyone can claim to know God and be a Christian. But unless you are actually doing good things in the name of Christ, it's just talk. Goodness is living out your faith by being good, or doing good works. Goodness is being friends with someone no one else likes; it's not cheating even though everyone else is; it's picking up the mess your brother or sister made. Goodness is the evidence that God has changed you. The world can talk like a Christian, but they will never behave like one. When you practice the fruit of goodness in your life, you show that your faith is more than words, but is a true change in your heart.

DAY 312

Faithfulness

But the fruit of the Spirit is love, joy, peace, patience, kindness, goodness, faithfulness. . . . Now those who belong to Christ Jesus have crucified the flesh with its passions and desires. (Galatians 5:22, 24)

Lord, Your faithful love reaches to heaven, Your faithfulness to the clouds. (Psalm 36:5)

Faithfulness is doing what you say you're going to do. It means that when you commit to something, you will honor your commitment. Faithfulness is a fruit of the Spirit—one that the world needs to see. When it comes to promises, even sacred promises like marriage, the world is not faithful. It constantly bails when things get hard. In the world, promises shatter like glass. In Christ, we have the ability to stay strong even when things are hard. God is always faithful to us. He never abandons us and never lets us go. He always keeps His promises. In Him, we have this fruit of the Spirit, and we show the world that Christ has made a difference in our lives.

DAY 313

Gentleness

But the fruit of the Spirit is love, joy, peace, patience, kindness, goodness, faithfulness, gentleness, and self-control. The law is not against such things. Now those who belong to Christ Jesus have crucified the flesh with its passions and desires. (Galatians 5:22–24)

Have you ever had to play a game with boys in gym class? Unless you're a tough girl (girl power!), it's the worst. Boys take the game so seriously and they don't care if you're a girl or not; they will hit you with the ball—sometimes on purpose. Generally when it comes to sports, boys are not very gentle. Gentleness is a fruit of the Spirit that has nothing to do with sports, and everything to do with how we treat people. Gentleness means you're careful in how you deal with people. You aren't quick to bash someone with your words. You think about other people's feelings before you speak. You never put someone down to make yourself look better. Christ was gentle in how He dealt with people. He was always considerate and never harsh with people, no matter how different they were. If you are a Christian, you will have gentleness in your life. You will care about others and treat them better than you treat yourself. We live in a world that is not gentle at all. By treating others with gentleness, you show the love of Christ to people who really need to see it.

DAY 314

Self-control

But the fruit of the Spirit is love, joy, peace, patience, kindness, goodness, faithfulness, gentleness, and self-control. The law is not against such things. Now those who belong to Christ Jesus have crucified the flesh with its passions and desires. (Galatians 5:22–24)

A little baby has no self-control. They eat as much as they want to eat, they cry when they want to cry, and they sleep when they want to sleep. Sadly, most of the world acts just like babies when it comes to self-control. They're mean when they get mad, they lie when it helps them, they spend money when they feel like it, and they follow every desire no matter how right or wrong. In Christ, self-control is a fruit of the Spirit. It just means that we deny ourselves something we really want in the moment because we trust God has something better for us. Self-control helps us guard our words, tell the truth, and be kind. It is a gift given to all followers of Christ so that we can show Him to the lost world. What chances have you already had to practice self-control? For starters, you woke up this morning, so you're already off to a great start. Let God help you practice the fruit of self-control today and you will receive His blessings.

Real Faith. Real Life.

Within every Christian girl is the power to live for God. The world is desperate to see Christian girls live for Christ with boldness. This section deals with practical ways we can live out our faith so the world will know the difference Christ makes in our lives.

DAY 315

More Than Words

Do nothing out of selfish ambition or conceit, but in humility consider others as more important than yourselves. (Philippians 2:3)

We live in a cutthroat world. That means that people will do whatever is necessary to get what they want, even if it means stealing, cheating, or crushing someone below them to make themselves look good. As followers of Christ, this should not be how we live. Instead of always wanting to be first, we let others go in front of us. Instead of craving attention, we help others get noticed. Instead of laughing at people who are different, we help the weak, the poor, and those who need friends. Our relationship with God isn't just something we talk about with words; it needs to be something we live. That means putting ourselves last and putting other people first. Ask God to show you one small way you can put someone else before yourself today.

DAY 316

Fully Connected, Signal: Strong

"I am the vine; you are the branches.
The one who remains in me and I in him produces
much fruit, because you can do nothing without me." (John 15:5)

You have to be near WiFi to connect to the Internet. The farther away you get, the worse of a connection you have and the slower the Internet runs. It's the same with God. If you want to live for God, you have to stay close to Him. The Bible says, "You can do nothing without me." If you try to do good works in your own power, you will fail. You need the power of God. The closer you get to God, the more you talk to Him, worship Him, and read His Word, the more He will do good things in you. The more you love God, the more power you will have to live for Him and stay away from temptation. He's the only power source for your life, so stay close to Him and you will have an instant connection to everything you need to live a godly life.

DAY 317

Perfect in Weakness

But he said to me, "My grace is sufficient for you,
for my power is perfected in weakness." Therefore, I will
most gladly boast all the more about my weaknesses,
so that Christ's power may reside in me. (2 Corinthians 12:9)

Imagine taking the hardest test your teacher could possibly give you. In the middle of the test, what if your teacher suddenly announced: "Class, you may copy the smartest student's work and turn it in as your own." You would be so happy! The whole class would pick the smartest girl's (or boy's) test to copy. The whole class would make an A, but everyone would know it was one student's work that earned the whole class a good grade. That student would get all the praise, attention, and gratitude. It's the same with God. Whatever the task, He can do it through you. Then He gets all the credit. Reach out to God. He loves to work through you and show Himself.

DAY
318

The Power of Discipline

*Instead, I discipline my body and bring it under strict control,
so that after preaching to others, I myself will not be disqualified.
(1 Corinthians 9:27)*

When you ride a bicycle, you don't ride into a thornbush, your neighbor's window, or a parked car and say, "That's just where the bike felt like going." That would be dumb. You tell your bike where to go. You tell it when to turn, when to stop, and when to avoid small children. In Christ, it's the same way with our actions. In Him, we have the power to control our bodies—they don't control us. We control what we say, how we act, and how we treat other people. God gives us self-control and the ability to discipline our bodies. The world doesn't have this control. They are slaves to their desires and emotions. Are you practicing that kind of control over your actions? Do you do whatever you feel like doing? Submit your life to God and draw close to Him. You will have control over your actions because God has control of your heart.

DAY 319

Accidentally a Ballerina

For the training of the body has limited benefit,
but godliness is beneficial in every way, since it holds promise for
the present life and also for the life to come. (1 Timothy 4:8)

What would happen right now if you were led on stage in a ballet costume and told to perform a dance for an auditorium full of people? Some could do it, but most of us would pinch ourselves to wake up from that nightmare. Why can't we dance ballet? Because we haven't practiced. If you're a dancer, you know that it takes years to get good. You have to practice several times a week. You have to develop muscles you didn't know you had. You have to get the right shoes, the right outfit, and the right instructor.

It's the same in our walks with God. We can't just walk out the door and expect to be like Christ. Becoming a godly girl takes a lot of training. We must build our spiritual muscle and practice godliness. We study the Word of God, obey our parents, and make our attitude like Jesus. What happens when we mess up? Well, if you've ever danced, you know that you mess up a lot before you learn the routine. When we mess up, we get up and keep going. It's a joyful journey, but one that takes 100 percent of who we are every day. When it comes to the Christian life, it's not about trying, but about training. Train to be like Christ.

DAY 320

Nobody Wants to Be the Sun

For everything was created by him, in heaven and on earth, the visible and the invisible, whether thrones or dominions or rulers or authorities—all things have been created through him and for him.
(Colossians 1:16)

At some point, every girl starts to think the sun doesn't exist. That's because she thinks that she sits at the center of the universe and all the planets spin around her. Seriously, every girl goes through a selfish, it's-all-about-me stage even if she never realizes it. As followers of Christ, we have to fight this me-focused attitude. When you think everything is all about you, you have a selfish attitude about your time, your parents' money, your friends, and your actions. You think everyone exists to make you happy. Instead of this selfish attitude, remember that God made the entire world, and He alone is king. Spend energy serving your family, serving your siblings and friends, and most of all seeking to please the Lord. Don't freak out when something doesn't go your way or you don't get what you want. It's really freeing to remember you're not in charge. Let Christ be the center of your world and put yourself last.

DAY 321

Seeing the World Through Thankful Eyes

Devote yourselves to prayer;
stay alert in it with thanksgiving. (Colossians 4:2)

We usually think about being thankful one time a year when there's a big turkey sitting in front of us. We quickly name off our blessings so we can get to eating. Actually, a thankful heart is so important all year. Instead of focusing on what you don't have, create a thankful heart by praising God for all the blessings He's already given you. Keep a thankful journal and list your blessings. Then when you feel bad, you can check it to see how blessed you really are. A thankful heart will change how you see the world and how you see your stuff. It also acts like a shield to fight off selfishness. A thankful heart cannot feel jealous or incomplete. Ask God to open your eyes to the blessings He's given you today.

DAY 322

Grow Up

Although by this time you ought to be teachers,
you need someone to teach you the basic principles of God's
revelation again. You need milk, not solid food. (Hebrews 5:12)

Have you ever met a ten-year-old girl who still drank from a bottle, slept in a crib, or rode in a car seat? Um, no. If you ever saw a girl acting like this, you'd want to tell her to grow up. Ten-year-olds are not babies. Sometimes, though, we do the same thing in our walks with God. When we first came to Christ, we were baby Christians. But the more time we spend with God, the more we grow in our faith. If you still struggle with the same things you struggled with as a baby Christian (lying, stealing, using bad language), you might need to grow up a little spiritually. Nobody wants to stay a baby. What are ways you have grown in your walk with God? If you are a new Christian, how do you want to grow as you follow God? There's nothing wrong with acting like a baby when you are a baby. But when enough time has passed, we need to show signs of growing up and moving spiritually from baby things to more mature things.

Math Homework for the Glory of Jesus

Whether you eat or drink, or whatever you do,
do everything for the glory of God. (1 Corinthians 10:31)

It's hard to see how learning fractions in math or recognizing direct objects in English will make a difference in your life. The truth is that not everything you learn in school will radically change your life. In Christ, however, that doesn't matter. We're supposed to do everything to the glory of God. That includes homework, school work, tests, and projects. Whether you're dissecting a frog in science or eating lunch with friends (hopefully not right afterwards), you are supposed to do it for the glory of God. You can honor God at school by doing your best work, being kind to teachers, and by being on time. These might seem like small things to you, but they make a difference. So instead of asking, "Why do I have to do this?" ask, "How can I bring glory to God while I do this?" It will bring a lot less stress and a lot more joy to your day—even when you're doing fractions.

DAY 324

Jars of Clay

Now we have this treasure in clay jars, so that this extraordinary power may be from God and not from us. (2 Corinthians 4:7)

Have you ever seen a movie where the princess or prince dresses up in commoner's clothes to escape the palace? Just because the princess wears shabby clothes and hides her crown doesn't mean she's not a princess; she just disguises her power to blend in. You might not realize it, but if you follow Christ, you walk around with the very power and presence of the almighty God inside of you at all times. The very same power that raised Christ from the dead is inside you. Scripture calls this having treasure in jars of clay, meaning you have a very great power in you, a regular girl. That way, when God works in your life, He gets all the credit, not you. You might not feel like royalty, but you are a daughter of the King. Don't be fooled by thinking you're ordinary. God lives inside you and is ready to work through you in the world.

DAY 325

Innocent in Evil, Wise in Serving

Brothers and sisters, don't be childish in your thinking, but be infants in regard to evil and adult in your thinking. (1 Corinthians 14:20)

There is no one more selfish than a child. If you have a younger brother or sister, you totally understand that. In this verse, Paul tells us to stop thinking like children. Children want their needs met and they think the whole world revolves around them. It's time for us to start serving others and stop demanding our own way. The only way we should be like children is in our innocence. Babies do not have an appetite for evil; they don't gossip or lie. They don't bully anyone or use swear words. We are to be innocent as well, keeping our eyes and minds far from the things of the world. It's time to stop thinking like a child and grow up in Christ, while at the same time staying innocent toward the evil in the world.

Race for the Prize

Don't you know that the runners in a stadium all race,
but only one receives the prize? Run in such a way to win the prize.
(1 Corinthians 9:24)

Some girls just aren't competitive. They don't care who wins as long as everyone has a good time. For the rest of us, we like to win. If we're going to play the game, we want to come in first. When it comes to our faith, Paul tells us to run like we're trying to win the prize. Our faith is not a passive, braid-your-hair-on-the-bleachers kind of faith. It demands all of who we are, our whole hearts, and our whole minds. We're supposed to spend our lives living for God, serving other people, and sharing the gospel. Although faith isn't a competition, there is definitely a prize at the end—heaven and eternity with Jesus. If you're feeling tired in your faith, come to God for energy. You were made to run the race of faith with passion and purpose. Run for the prize.

DAY 327

Favored

I have sought your favor with all my heart; be gracious to me according to your promise. (Psalm 119:58)

You know the girl in your class who is a total teacher's pet? She says everything the teacher wants to hear and is a perfect little angel whenever adults are looking. Even though this behavior is annoying, it actually feels pretty good when adults are pleased with us. We all love to get encouragement from our coaches, our parents, and our teachers. Even more valuable than their praise, however, is the praise of God. God loves to pour His blessings and favor on you when you seek Him. He never overlooks your good actions. He always praises a right choice, even when no one else sees it. When you seek His favor, you will find it. As important as it is to please the adults in your life, seek to please the Lord too. He is ready to bless you and to pour His favor on your life.

DAY 328

Just Like the Ant

Go to the ant, you slacker!
Observe its ways and become wise. (Proverbs 6:6)

Imagine sitting on the couch all day watching movies, eating junk food, and sleeping. Some days, nothing seems better. There's nothing wrong with a lazy day now and then, but if you're always lazy, the Bible says you will be miserable. We were made for work. God has a job for us to do and wants to accomplish things through us. Laziness is the exact same thing as selfishness because it's all about you. Hard work and godliness go together. You will never find someone truly godly who is also lazy. If you struggle with laziness, the best thing to do is to get off the couch, turn off the computer, and ask your parents how you can help them. After they recover from shock, they will be proud of your willingness to work hard for the family.

DAY 329

Unbreakable

*Put no more trust in a mere human, who has only the breath
in his nostrils. What is he really worth? (Isaiah 2:22)*

Your trust is a precious gift to give away. When you give it to the wrong person, that trust shatters into a million pieces. We've all had our trust betrayed by someone who was unworthy to have it. The Bible tells us to stop trusting people. That doesn't mean you build a wall around your heart to keep people out. It just means that you shouldn't put all your hope and all your trust in any one person. God alone is worthy to hold your trust. He will never betray you and never break your trust. He knows what you need and He knows the plans for your life. Put your complete trust in Him, and then you're free to trust others too. When people disappoint you, you no longer have to be devastated because your God will never disappoint you.

DAY 330

Unable to Trap

The administrators and satraps, therefore, kept trying to find a charge against Daniel regarding the kingdom. But they could find no charge or corruption, for he was trustworthy, and no negligence or corruption was found in him. (Daniel 6:4)

In the Old Testament, evil leaders tried to trap Daniel, a godly man. They tried so hard to find a flaw in his character. But they couldn't find it. He was totally trustworthy. What about you? If someone tried to find sin in your life, would they have an easy time? If someone had a record of every word you've spoken this week, would they find encouraging words used to build up others? No one is perfect, but realize that if you claim to know God, the world really needs to see those claims lived out in your life. They need to see a changed life. Think carefully about your actions and glorify God in everything you do so that no one can bring a charge of sin against you.

DAY 331

I Will Forgive You

. . . bearing with one another and forgiving one another
if anyone has a grievance against another. Just as the Lord
has forgiven you, so you are also to forgive. (Colossians 3:13)

Imagine getting accidentally handcuffed to your brother or sister, right after a huge fight. Could there be anything worse? You're already furious, and now you have to drag them around everywhere you go. There's no relief, no escape. Wherever you go, there they are. That's what unforgiveness does to you. When someone hurts you, and you don't forgive, you chain yourself to that person. You hold them hostage so wherever you go, you carry the weight of their betrayal. When you forgive someone, you unchain yourself and hand them over to God. You quit making them owe you, and you give their debt to God. Forgiveness doesn't mean you trust them again. It doesn't even mean you have to be friends again right away. It just means that God is responsible for justice, not you. Be quick to forgive someone. Don't hold grudges or let bitterness grow. When you forgive, you're setting yourself free, not the other person. When you were at your worst, God forgave you. Remember that kind of forgiveness, and give it to other people.

DAY 332

Leave Your Stuff Behind

*They brought the boats to land, left everything,
and followed him. (Luke 5:11)*

When traveling, girls usually like to pack a lot of stuff. Even if it's just one night, we need a suitcase full of things. We need clothes, shoes, PJs, makeup, blow dryer, straightener, our phone, hair products, lotion, contact solution, and a bunch of other stuff because you never know if you'll need it, right? It's the exact opposite when we come to Christ. When you come to Jesus for salvation, you don't take anything with you. You leave behind your bags filled with anger, lies, and bad attitudes. You don't carry your pride, your forgiveness, or your selfishness. You even leave behind the good stuff too—your dreams, your plans, and your desires. You come to Him totally empty-handed, and He gives you a brand-new life, with everything you need for godliness. Are you still trying to carry some of your old luggage? Are you clinging to a certain sin or bad attitude from your past? Let it go. God's life for you is so much better—no heavy lifting required.

DAY 333

Never Forget

I will remember the LORD's works; yes,
I will remember your ancient wonders. (Psalm 77:11)

As girls, sometimes we suffer from short-term memory loss. We're really good at remembering when a friend made us mad a month ago, but we tend to forget the good things she did for us just today. We do the same thing with God. We're great at asking him to do things for us, but slow to remember when He answers those prayers. We have to remember the blessings of God. He has come through for us in so many ways. Those past blessings can encourage us when we face a trial in the future. So talk about what God has done for you in your life. When He answers a prayer, write it down in a journal. Then when you're feeling sad, you can go back and remember. The same God who answered your prayers in the past will answer them in the future. There is power in remembering. The God who came through for you before will come through for you again. Never forget.

DAY 334

Be Still

"Be still, and know that I am God." (Psalm 46:10 NIV)

So much noise rings in our ears every day. We hear the shouts of teachers, TV shows, movies, commercials, and our friends. In our down time, we cram headphones into our ears or get on the computer. In all the noise, it can be difficult to hear the voice of God. God tells us to be still and know that He is God. It's so important to find the time to shut off every noise in your life so that you can hear from God. A few minutes every day, go before the Lord in silence. Let the reality of who He is wash over you. He loves you so much. One minute spent with Him can accomplish more than a whole day listening to the noise of the world. Be still and know that He is God, and He will be lifted up and glorified through your life.

DAY 335

Nothing Else Matters

*More than that, I also consider everything to be a loss
in view of the surpassing value of knowing Christ Jesus my Lord.
Because of him I have suffered the loss of all things and consider
them as dung, so that I may gain Christ. (Philippians 3:8)*

If you want to be on a winning sports team, you have to make sacrifices. You have to wake up early on Saturdays, run laps, do drills, and sweat a lot. As long as you remember the main goal, those sacrifices don't seem too important, but if you lose focus, you get frustrated. In the Bible, Paul reminds us that the main thing about our Christian life is to know Jesus more. Everything else fails in comparison. God doesn't just want us to go to church and be a good girl; He wants to capture us with the knowledge of who He is. His sacrifice on the cross puts everything in perspective for us. When we focus on knowing Him, the little sacrifices we have to make don't matter anymore. Keep your mind and heart focused on the main thing: knowing Jesus more. Don't get so distracted by the duties of a Christian that you forget the joy of knowing Him as Savior.

DAY 336

Never Out of Minutes

In him we have boldness and confident
access through faith in him. (Ephesians 3:12)

Have you ever waited in line to meet someone famous? When you finally get to them, you're so nervous and silly, you say two words, get an autograph, and then it's over. We don't have to wait in a line to see God. He always has more than two minutes for us. The Bible says you can approach Him with confidence. You have constant access to your Father—you never run out of minutes. You never have to be afraid or worry how He's going to receive you. Take advantage of this access, but don't take it for granted. Meet with God daily; pray to Him when you need Him or just to tell Him how awesome He is. He is the most famous, most glorious, most worthy of our attention, and He loves to spend time with you. Don't miss His presence in your life today.

DAY
337

Wiped Out

*Therefore, strengthen your tired hands and weakened knees,
and make straight paths for your feet, so that what is lame
may not be dislocated but healed instead. (Hebrews 12:12–13)*

Have you ever gone to school totally exhausted? Maybe you stayed up too late the night before and you're struggling to keep your eyes open in class. You just want to crawl into a cozy corner of the room and drift off to sleep. When it comes to living for Christ, sometimes we feel tired and weak. Maybe you're tired of always doing the right thing or always being the good girl. Maybe you're sick of being the dependable one. When you feel exhausted spiritually, run to God. He is the only source of energy. He will awaken your heart and remind you of how much He loves you. Like a giant cup of coffee, He will give you energy to keep living for Him. When you try to be good apart from a relationship with God, you will get exhausted and you will fail. Spend time with God and let Him pour His love, peace, and joy back into your life so you can live for Him with full energy and with the strength only He can give.

DAY 338

In the Presence of God

The Lord answered her, "Martha, Martha, you are worried and upset about many things, but one thing is necessary. Mary has made the right choice, and it will not be taken away from her." (Luke 10:41–42)

Sometimes we get so busy we don't have time to sit with Jesus. God loves our hard work and the good things we do with our families and friends. But He also knows that when we're busy without spending time with Him, we get stressed out. He's the one who gives us the power to live for Him. When you sit in the presence of God in prayer or in worship or just in silence, He can pour His love on you. The busier you are, the more you need to spend time in the presence of God. Don't miss your time with Him. It will bless you and fill you with the energy and patience to accomplish everything He planned for you that day.

Every Word Matters

Get two girls together, and you're likely to hear any conversation about any subject. The only thing you won't hear is silence. Girls talk a lot, and we have power in our words. In this section, we learn the power of our words and how to take every word we speak captive before Christ.

DAY 339

About Ourselves

I will praise you because I have been remarkably and wondrously made. Your works are wondrous, and I know this very well. (Psalm 139:14)

She talks about you behind your back. She points out all your flaws and dislikes how you look. She's quick to criticize you and slow to find anything good. Do you know who this mean person is? YOU! You are the biggest critic of yourself. As girls, we are so hard on ourselves. We find our flaws and forget our beauty. We criticize how we look, and we're never good enough. It's time to stop being our own bully. It's time to see yourself as God sees you. He looks at you and is overcome with love. He is captivated by your beauty and delights in who you are. We must start seeing beauty in ourselves—physical and spiritual beauty. If we don't like ourselves, how can we trust God to love us? If you can't think of something positive to say, speak the words of Scripture over yourself. You were made by God. You were bought for the price of God's own Son. You have a purpose. You have gifts and talents. Refuse to put yourself down. You are the temple of the Holy Spirit, and you are beautiful.

DAY 340

Behind Someone's Back

*A gossip goes around revealing a secret,
but a trustworthy person keeps a confidence. (Proverbs 11:13)*

When was the last time you got sick from a friend? It doesn't feel good. You probably took that same germ and passed it right along to another friend. Before you know it, you've all passed around the same virus and you're all feeling yucky. This is how gossip works. When you hear a crazy story about someone else—a story that has nothing to do with you—and you tell other people, it's like spreading around a virus. One by one, the sickness spreads as the story gets passed around. Everyone who gossips plays a part in the sickness. Instead of spreading someone else's story, tell it to God and pray for the person. Don't take joy in someone else's bad news. By keeping your mouth shut, you stop the spread of gossip, and you stop the spread of hurt and pain to yourself and your friends.

DAY 341

To Other People

Blessing and cursing come out of the same mouth. My brothers and sisters, these things should not be this way. Does a spring pour out sweet and bitter water from the same opening? (James 3:10–11)

Have you ever had a two-faced sibling? She acts one way when she's around you, but as soon as mom and dad are around, she's a perfect little angel. They can't see why you'd ever get mad at her. In Christ, we are called to live totally, completely, and only for Him. We no longer act one way around our friends at school and another way around our friends at church. God demands all of us, our whole hearts. It's the same with our language. We can't praise God at church and then bash our enemies the next day. It doesn't work like that. The Bible says that fresh water and salt water can't come from the same source. In the same way, evil words and encouraging words can't come from the same mouth. If you submit your heart to God, He will clean up your language. I know it's hard, and it's not something that can be accomplished all at once. But the closer you get to God, the more your words will reflect His. And you will be a source of fresh, life-giving water to everyone you meet.

DAY 342

Words Used as Poison

Every kind of animal, bird, reptile, and fish is tamed
and has been tamed by humankind, but no one can tame the tongue.
It is a restless evil, full of deadly poison. (James 3:7–8)

The last time I checked, humans didn't have poisonous bites like a snake. But the Bible says our tongues are full of deadly poison. James is talking about our words. Our words have more power than we could ever realize. They can be life-giving and healing, but they can also be poisonous. Things like gossip, negativity, and cursing spew poison and cut people down. When you encourage others, speak God's Word, and praise the Lord, you bring healing and you're a source of life to a hurting world. When you speak the gospel to someone, you could literally be helping change their eternal destiny. How are you using the power of your words? Ask God to capture every word you speak.

DAY 343

Our Words to God

*My mouth is full of praise and honor
to you all day long. (Psalm 71:8)*

When you're busy praising God with your words, you don't have room to bash other people. When you speak about God's love, His blessings, and His promises, you don't have time to be negative or whine. There's a reason God's Word tells us to praise Him all day. It's not because God's bored and needs something to listen do. When we use our words in praise to God, evil words cannot come from our mouths. Have you taken a bite of something you thought was sweet but it was actually salty? It's a shock to your system and you usually spit it out. It's the same with our words. When you're busy praising God, and hear something negative, you want to get rid of it quickly. When you hear a bad word or gossip, it shocks your heart and you know God is not pleased with it. You want it out of your life. Spend the day praising God out loud and in your mind. That way no evil words have a chance of dragging you down.

DAY 344

In Strong Emotion

But now, put away all the following:
anger, wrath, malice, slander, and filthy language
from your mouth. (Colossians 3:8)

When you feel a strong emotion, you want to use strong words. The world teaches us that the only way to convey strong emotions like anger or surprise is to use curse words. These words don't glorify God and have no positive impact on your life. Scripture tells us to put away filthy language. If you're in the habit of swearing, let God begin to break you of that habit. When you follow Christ, you wear His image and you show the world what it looks like to be a Christian. Your actions and your words prove your faith to be real. We cannot use the same words as the world and expect to look any different. God is able to purify your speech and give you the self-control you need to avoid curse words. Take every word captive before God and make Him pleased with every word that comes out of your mouth.

DAY 345

Power in Silence

When there are many words, sin is unavoidable,
but the one who controls his lips is prudent. (Proverbs 10:19)

Girls like to talk. It's how God made us. He must really love the sound of our voices because He hears them a lot. In the thousands of words we speak each day (oh, who are we kidding, each hour), we must be careful. Scripture teaches that where there are many words, sin is unavoidable. That doesn't mean we should stop talking, but we should make sure our words honor God. It also means that it's always wise to stop and think before you speak—especially if you're feeling upset. You can't take back something hurtful you've said, so it's always better just not to say it. Today, practice watching your words. Ask God to help every word you speak honor Him and build other people up. If you're in doubt, just don't say it.

DAY 346

When Words Cut Down

If you bite and devour one another, watch out,
or you will be consumed by one another. (Galatians 5:15)

Time to get real. As girls, we can be nasty with our words. We can use our words to rip another girl apart behind her back. When we're angry, our words can cut sharper than a blade. Gossip, cursing, and criticism can spew out of our mouths like poison. The truth is that we use our words to hurt those we love the most, our families. We have to grow up in Christ. Girls, we have to stop using our words to cut people down. Even when we're really upset, we have to give God control of our words. The Bible says that your words have great power. It's time to stop letting our words control us and to start controlling our words in the name of Jesus. What you speak to your little brother or sister matters. How you talk to your mom matters, and not just when you're happy, but when you're angry or upset. When Jesus died on the cross, He overcame sin and made us alive in Him. That includes the words we speak. Stop using words to attack, gossip, call names, and speak in anger. You are the words you speak, so make sure your words reflect Christ in everything you say.

DAY 347

When It's Time to Close Our Mouths

My dear brothers and sisters, understand this: Everyone should be quick to listen, slow to speak, and slow to anger. (James 1:19)

Sometimes the most encouraging thing we can do for a friend is just to shut our mouths. The world is full of people who are quick to share advice and give opinions, but the power of listening is rare. When you really listen to a sibling or a friend, you show them that they matter. When you let them talk, it's really a way of serving them. Sometimes all a friend needs is someone to listen to her, someone to show her that her thoughts matter. It's amazing how much you learn when you close your mouth. You start to see where people are coming from and what's in their hearts. You can also learn a lot from your parents by just listening to what they say. The next time you have the opportunity to listen, take advantage of it. Our world is full of people jumping to have their voice heard, but there are few people who listen. Recognize the beauty of listening. Listen to your friends, listen to your siblings, listen to your parents, and, most importantly, listen to God.

DAY 348

Speech Proves Salvation

If anyone thinks he is religious without controlling his tongue, his religion is useless and he deceives himself. (James 1:26)

"A good person produces good out of the good stored up in his heart. An evil person produces evil out of the evil stored up in his heart, for his mouth speaks from the overflow of the heart." (Luke 6:45)

The beautiful thing about walking with God is that He changes every part of you—not just your thoughts, not just your habits, and not just your relationships, but your whole being. He puts His Holy Spirit in your life who changes you from the inside out, and that includes your words. When you come to Christ, He gives you a new life—His life. He wants you to act like Him and that includes the words you speak. That's why James says that we must control our tongues. Maybe you can fake being a Christian for a little while, but your words will always prove who you really are. The beautiful thing about walking with God is that He will transform your speech. As you get closer to Him, you will notice if the words you say don't match your faith. You'll be convicted by things like lying, gossip, and swearing. God doesn't just change your speech; He changes your heart. If you follow Christ, you want to please Him. Submit your words to God and He will help your speech be a perfect mirror of what's in your heart.

DAY 349

Tell the Truth

How joyful is a person whom the Lᴏʀᴅ does not charge with iniquity and in whose spirit is no deceit! (Psalm 32:2)

Have you ever accidentally walked face-first into a spider web? It's disgusting! After screaming, you have to swat the web away several times because it's really sticky. You've heard that lying is like spinning a web. Every day you have the opportunity to spin a web of lies. You can lie to your teachers by cheating on your homework, or you can lie to friends about why you didn't call them back; you can lie to your parents, lie to your siblings, or lie to strangers. Lying usually gives you a quick way out of an uncomfortable situation. It offers an easy chance to make yourself look good. But before you know it, you've spun a web that will trap you quicker than a fly to a spider. The Bible tells us that lying is wrong. It promises a quick way out, but in the long run it really hurts you. Lying damages your character and hurts your relationship with God. Choose to tell the truth, even if it means you get in trouble, even if it means you get a lower grade. Nothing is worth sacrificing your integrity. Today when you're faced with the chance to spin a lie, choose the truth instead. You might feel a little pain, but you will honor God and be free from a web of lies.

Fresh Out of the Ordinary

In Christ, we live brand-new lives. This section focuses on the extraordinary things God wants to do as He lives through us.

DAY 350

Love Your Enemies

"You have heard that it was said, Love your neighbor and hate your enemy. But I tell you, love your enemies and pray for those who persecute you." (Matthew 5:43–44)

We all know someone we just don't like. That person may be in your class at school, ride your bus, or even be in your family. When you clash with someone, the last thing you feel like doing is being nice. It's even harder to actually love them. But in Christ, that's exactly what we're supposed to do. God's Word tells us to love our enemies. For some of us, God may as well have told us to fly through the air and give our enemies a million dollars (it ain't gonna happen). Seriously, in Christ we have the power to love the people who annoy us most. Not in your own strength, but through Him, you can see your enemies differently and have compassion on them. Ask God to help you see that person the way He sees him or her. How others treat you should not define how you treat them in return. You are in Christ, and you have the power to love no matter what. Let Christ love your enemies through you.

DAY 351

Share Your Stuff

Now the entire group of those who believed were of one heart and mind, and no one claimed that any of his possessions was his own, but instead they held everything in common. (Acts 4:32)

One of the extraordinary things we do as Christians is to share our stuff. We recognize that everything we have is God's, so we enjoy sharing what we have with others. We aren't stingy or slow to give because we know God has already given us so much. One of the first things you have to teach a baby is how to share. That's because babies are born selfish, demanding attention, and clinging to their possessions. When we were baby Christians, we were selfish too, but the closer we get to God, the more we want to share our possessions. In fact, you can tell how close someone is to God by how they view their stuff. People who have spent time with God want to be generous with their things. Practice sharing your stuff this week with your siblings, your friends, and even people you don't like. The act of giving changes our hearts and shows the world that we're different.

DAY 352

Die to Ourselves

*"Whoever tries to make his life secure will lose it,
and whoever loses his life will preserve it." (Luke 17:33)*

Another crazy thing we do as Christians is die to ourselves. The world fights hard to stay alive. They cling to their pride, their desires, and their plans. When we come to Christ, however, we die—not physically, but spiritually. All of us for all of Him. In fact, Jesus Himself teaches that if we want to save our lives, we will lose it. If we lose our lives for God, we will find them. This is not a riddle, but the truth about the Christian life. God loves you so much He will not let you live in your sinful self. He won't let anything survive that is part of the old you—your pride, your evil thoughts, your negativity, your selfishness, your bad attitude. He wants to kill it all so you can come alive in Him. Then He gives you a new life, a new mind, a new heart, and a new purpose. Why would you want to keep something alive that was already dead to begin with? We serve a God who demands our death, spiritually speaking, so we can come to Him and find new life.

Walk on Water

*And climbing out of the boat, Peter started walking
on the water and came toward Jesus. (Matthew 14:29)*

Maybe we can't exactly walk on water, but we can still do extraordinary things for God. If you know Christ, girl, you are anything but ordinary. The Spirit of the living God lives inside you. You have the mind of Christ. You have the power to do the will and the work of God in your every day life. Often the miracles we see are invisible, but more powerful than anything we could see with our eyes. Christ wants to love people through you. He wants to use you to introduce your friends to Him. He empowers you to avoid sin that the world can't resist. You have power to love your enemies. You can even have love, joy, and peace in the middle of the worst time in your life. Only God can do this for you. So the next time you're feeling ordinary, kick that feeling in the face. You are an extraordinary girl in Christ, destined to do great things for your Savior.

DAY 354

Hang Out with Unpopular People

"On the contrary, when you host a banquet, invite those who are poor, maimed, lame, or blind." (Luke 14:13)

Jesus sure knows how to send an e-vite. When He throws a party, He invites the poor, the sick, the unpopular—basically all the losers in town. Why? Because that's who He came to save. The world wants to be around cool people. They chaise after the rich, the famous, the popular, and the beautiful. Jesus did the opposite. He loved those the world overlooked. We're supposed to love like that. We see the hurting and the broken people around us and reach out to them. We make friends with people who aren't cool or popular so we can show Christ to them. The closer you get to God, the more joy you will get out of loving the needy people around you. Who around you needs your compassion? Who needs to be invited to be around you and to feel wanted? Love them with the love of Christ.

DAY 355

Worth a Thousand Words

Then Mary took a pound of perfume, pure and expensive nard, anointed Jesus's feet, and wiped his feet with her hair. So the house was filled with the fragrance of the perfume. (John 12:3)

If only Jesus had Instagram. This picture would definitely be one of His favorites. One woman, an outcast in society, took her most valuable possession, a jar of expensive perfume, and poured it out on Jesus' feet. Then in an act of worship, she washed His feet with her hair. To the people in the room, it looked like Mary was crazy. They wondered why Mary would waste such an expensive gift on Jesus' feet. But Jesus understood. This woman poured out everything she had to Jesus. She worshipped Him in a radical way. She held nothing back. She didn't care what anyone else thought about her. That's exactly what we're supposed to do. God wants us to love Him with our whole hearts, so that we hold nothing back from Him. The picture of Mary washing Jesus' feet with her hair is a powerful example of how we are to live for God. Give Him everything you are, and don't let the world make you ashamed. Your God loves you and deserves your worship.

Overthrow the Drama Queen

You never have to guess how a girl feels. We are a waterfall of emotions. God created us to feel deeply and passionately because He Himself feels deep emotion. This section focuses on celebrating your emotions but not letting them control you or cause you to sin.

DAY 356

Please Step Off the Roller Coaster

I don't say this out of need, for I have learned to be content in whatever circumstances I find myself. (Philippians 4:11)

As girls, we live much of our lives on a roller coaster of emotions. I think God must delight in a little drama because He made us this way. Sometimes the roller coaster gets a little out of hand when we're super happy one day and bitterly depressed the next. Paul said he had learned to be content no matter what—he actually wrote this verse from prison. There is a secret to always having peace, always having joy, and always feeling content. It is the presence of God. True contentment isn't a place or a circumstance. It isn't having tons of money or popularity or external beauty. True joy is knowing God and living in His love. When you truly experience the intimacy of God, no bad event or painful circumstance can steal your joy. So the next time you're tempted to dive off the cliff of a bad day, remember that no one has the power to steal your joy when you live in the presence of God.

The Girl Who Caught on Fire

A fool gives full vent to his anger,
but a wise person holds it in check. (Proverbs 29:11)

Have you ever seen something accidentally catch on fire? Maybe you dropped a match on the ground or left something in the oven too long and it started smoking. Immediately your only thought is to put out the fire before it spreads. What if you did nothing? What if you just let the burning match spread or left the burning food in the oven? That fire would destroy everything. It's the same with anger. When you get angry, it's just like that spark leaping out of the fire. It will eventually explode into a raging flame. The smallest spark of anger can grow into a fierce rage if we don't take it to God. Scripture doesn't say that a fool gets angry; it says that a fool gives full vent to his anger. If you're constantly flying off the handle in huge dramatic bursts of anger, that behavior is not of God. Keep your temper in check. When you feel that fire start to grow, pour water on it by praying, reading Scripture, or talking to a godly friend or parent.

DAY 358

For the Joy Set before You

For the kingdom of God is not eating and drinking, but righteousness, peace, and joy in the Holy Spirit. (Romans 14:17)

In the presence of God you find joy that the world can't make. God is able to fill you with true, lasting joy that is deeper and more powerful than any situation you can encounter. This joy makes you brave. It makes you generous. It makes you face the day with peace. Did you know that joy isn't an accident? God created you to desire joy, and He's the one who can make it happen. Scripture says that for the joy set before Him, Jesus endured the cross. Jesus had a joy so powerful that it helped Him endure a horrible death. Are you experiencing that joy? True joy doesn't always mean you're having a great day or you don't have any problems. It just means that even in the middle of your problems you have peace in God. Taste and see that the Lord is good. Experience His joy, and it will sustain you through whatever day you face.

DAY 359

Please Say No One Saw That

May the Lord of peace himself give you peace always in every way. The Lord be with all of you. (2 Thessalonians 3:16)

Maybe you tripped and fell flat on your face. Maybe your friend blurted out your worst secret. We all have embarrassing moments. Your face turns red and you want to turn invisible and run away. Did you know that God actually cares about your embarrassing moments? He doesn't laugh at you or make you feel shame. Take those moments to Him and He will help you deal with them. He will give you the courage you need to go back into the classroom or face your friends again. He might even help you see the funny side of your moment—at least eventually. Trust Him with every part of your day—even your most horrific embarrassing moment because He is trustworthy.

DAY 360

Are You Kidding Me?

I pour out my complaint before him;
I reveal my trouble to him. (Psalm 142:2)

You didn't make the team. You studied hard but still didn't make a good grade. Your friend made you angry. Disappointment happens to every girl. It's painful, and it can make us feel alone. God wants us to come to Him with all our disappointments. He loves you so much that He wants to be the first one you run to when you're sad. He will wrap His arms around you and remind you that you are His daughter. Unlike everyone else, He knows exactly how you feel and how to make you feel better. Trust God with your disappointment, and He will heal your heart.

DAY 361

A Thousand Broken Pieces

My spirit is broken. (Job 17:1)

Some things are more serious than a bad hair day or a broken nail. Some things in life really hurt us. Things like the death of a loved one, disease, or divorce cut us deeply and leave us broken. When this happens, we can't just pick up the pieces and move on. The truth is that God is close to the brokenhearted. He holds you in His arms, even through the pain. He has not abandoned you. In fact, He knows the number of your tears and He sees each one. Cling to Him, sweet girl. Run to Him for comfort. His arms are safe. Although you don't understand why it happened, you can trust God. He will stay by your side and guide you through the pain. He is the God who mends our broken hearts, even when they seem too wounded to be fixed. You are His daughter and He is your Father. Pour your heart out to Him and trust Him to meet your needs.

DAY 362

The Weight of Worry

"Therefore I tell you: Don't worry about your life,
what you will eat or what you will drink; or about your body,
what you will wear. Isn't life more than food and
the body more than clothing?" (Matthew 6:25)

Have you ever tried to walk around with a little cousin or sibling on your back? Before you know it, you're out of breath and begging them to get off. They get heavy fast. That's what worry does to us. Worry acts like a giant weight on our backs, slowing us down and making us miserable. The worst part is that it's pointless. It doesn't help our future, and it doesn't help us to wait in the present. God knows this. We were not created to worry. The next time you worry—over school, tryouts, friendships, money, or boys—stop, before it weighs you down. Remember the promises of God to love us and protect us. Let God pry that worry weight off of you and replace it with faith.

Mean Girls

We all know a mean girl. We see her at school, in the neighborhood, or sometimes in the mirror. This section teaches us to deal with a mean girl without becoming one ourselves.

DAY 363

The Girl I Want to Trip

Friends, do not avenge yourselves; instead, leave room for God's wrath, because it is written, Vengeance belongs to me; I will repay, says the Lord. (Romans 12:19)

She pushes everyone around. She makes fun of kids who aren't popular. She picks on everyone weaker than her. Nobody likes a mean girl. These bullies live to make other people miserable. When you have a mean girl at your school or in your neighborhood, how should you react? Immediately tell your parents. They need to know if anyone is picking on you or another student. Then together you can tell your teacher. You never have to tolerate abuse from a bully, but don't get revenge. Stand up for yourself, but don't take the evil a step further. You never want to stoop to a mean girl's level or become a bully yourself. Tell your parents, stand up to the bully, but trust God when it comes to getting even.

DAY 364

The Mean Girl Is Me

May the Lord make your love increase and overflow for each other and for everyone else, just as ours does for you.
(1 Thessalonians 3:12 NIV)

Sometimes the mean girl is you. Maybe you struggle with threatening others or pushing people around. Maybe you're afraid if you weren't mean then no one would take you seriously. Whatever the reason, God is able to heal you. He never created you to be a mean girl, to your friends, in your neighborhood, or to your little siblings. God desires you to know Him and let Him fill you with His love and peace. Ask for God's forgiveness and ask for forgiveness from the people you've bullied. No one likes to be a bully. But it takes more than wanting to stop. It takes the power of Christ in your life to break down the walls. Surrender to Christ and trust Him to change you. He will set you free from the miserable life of a bully.

DAY 365

The Girl Who Gets Bullied

Blessed are those who have regard for the weak;
the Lord delivers them in times of trouble. (Psalm 41:1 NIV)

There's always a girl who attracts bullies. She may look a little different or wear clothes that aren't in style. She usually doesn't have many friends. Bullies love picking on girls like this because they don't fight back. Until now. When you follow Christ, God's Word says you are to help the weak. You have God's eyes to see those who are in trouble and you are to go to their rescue. You can tell a teacher or stand up to the bullies yourself, but do you know the most powerful weapon that defends a weak girl? Be her friend. Let her know she's not alone, and although everyone else may have abandoned her, you will not abandon her. Live out your faith and be friends with the unpopular girls. Sit by her at lunch or on the bus. Let her know she matters to you. It will honor God, and it will bring more joy to this girl than you could ever imagine to know she's not alone.